Practical Guide to Epilepsy Awareness and Control

Carter A. Garcia

All rights reserved. Copyright © 2023 Carter A. Garcia

Funny helpful tips:

Stay connected with 5G technology; its faster speeds and lower latency are transforming communication and IoT.

Your story is a legacy; pen it with authenticity and pride.

*Practical Guide to Epilepsy Awareness and Control :
Unlocking the Secrets of Epilepsy: A Comprehensive Handbook
for Understanding and Managing Seizures*

Life advices:

Stay updated with advancements in gesture recognition; it's enhancing device interactions without touch.

Diversify your reading list; exposing yourself to various genres and cultures broadens your perspective.

Introduction

This book offers valuable insights and information about this neurological disorder. The guide begins with a brief history of epilepsy, followed by a clarification of the medical professionals who treat epilepsy and debunking myths associated with the condition.

Understanding epilepsy is crucial, as it is a physical disorder and not a mental disease. The guide covers various types of seizures, including focal seizures and generalized seizures, and emphasizes the importance of recognizing and addressing seizure recurrence.

Diagnosing epilepsy is explored in detail, with a focus on identifying different causes, including neurological and non-neurological factors. The guide encourages readers to take action and seek appropriate medical attention for their condition, considering febrile seizures and distinguishing them from epilepsy.

When it comes to treatment, the guide delves into the use of medications and the possible drug interactions that can occur. It highlights the need to explore alternative treatments, including clinical trials and out-of-the-mainstream therapies, for those who may not respond well to standard medication.

For some individuals with epilepsy, surgery may be an option. The guide provides insights into epilepsy surgery, the different types available, and potential complications. It stresses the importance of considering surgery carefully and seeking second opinions when necessary.

The guide further explores epilepsy in specific demographics, such as children, seniors, and women. It sheds light on the causes and treatment of childhood epilepsy, parental concerns, epilepsy in seniors, and the impact of epilepsy on women's fertility and pregnancy.

Living with epilepsy can present challenges, and the guide offers advice on navigating social relationships, both casual and intimate. It encourages individuals with epilepsy to take action and actively participate in society while managing their condition effectively.

In conclusion, this book provides a comprehensive and compassionate resource for understanding, managing, and living with epilepsy. By dispelling myths and offering evidence-based insights, the guide aims to empower individuals with epilepsy to lead fulfilling lives while managing their condition effectively.

Contents

Epilepsy 1
   A Brief History of Epilepsy 2
   Who Treats Epilepsy? 4
   The Myths 5
   What You Should Know 10
Epilepsy Is a Physical Disorder, Not a Mental Disease 12
   Types of Seizures 16
   Focal Seizures 17
   Generalized Seizures 24
   Recurrence of Seizures 32
   What You Should Know 33
Diagnosing Epilepsy 35
   Types of Causes 44
   Neurological Causes of Epilepsy 45
   Non-Neurological Conditions 47
   Take Action 48
   Febrile Seizures 48
   Not All Seizures Are Epilepsy 49
   What You Should Know 50
Treating Epilepsy 51
   Take Action 59
   Drug Interactions 62
   When Does Medication End? 62
   What You Should Know 63

When Medications Aren't Working 64
    How Are Drugs Switched When One Drug Isn't Working? 68
    Should More Than One Drug Be Used?...69
    What If Dosages Have Been Adjusted and/or Drugs Have Been Switched and There Is Still No Improvement? 69
    Alternative Treatments 70
    Are Clinical Trials a Good Option?..73
    What about Out-of-the-Mainstream Therapies?......................................74
    What Everyone Should Know 75

Epilepsy Surgery 76
    Considering Surgery Is Not a Commitment to Having the Surgery 83
    Second Opinions for Epilepsy Surgery 84
    Invasive Testing...86
    Types of Epilepsy Surgery..87
    Complications from Surgery 90
    Take Action..93
    What to Expect after Surgery 93
    Why Surgery Might Not Work...94
    What If Surgery Is Not an Option?...94
    Are Clinical Trials a Good Option?...95
    What You Should Know 95

Epilepsy in Children, Seniors, and Women 97
    Causes of Childhood Epilepsy...107
    Treatment of Epilepsy in Children 108
    Multiple Conditions...109
    Parental Concerns about the Future...110
    Issues at Three Stages of Childhood..111

What You Should Know	115
Epilepsy in Seniors	116
What You Should Know	123
Epilepsy in Women	124
Epilepsy, Sex, and Fertility	128
Contraception and Planning Your Family	130
Pregnancy	132
Epilepsy and Baby Care	133
What You Should Know	134
Living withEpilepsy	135
Living in the World	142
Take Action	144
Social Relationships—Casual and Intimate	145
What You Should Know	146
Conclusion	148

Chapter 1

Epilepsy

The History and the Myths

There are many myths and misconceptions in the public mind that often have a negative impact on people with epilepsy as well as on their families and friends. The facts about epilepsy pose sufficient challenges without creating even more issues arising out of errors, speculation, and misstatements. In this chapter, I will try to correct some of those misunderstandings.

What follows is a quick historical overview of epilepsy, showing how the thinking about this condition has evolved over time. I will address some of the specific myths about epilepsy and provide the truth, which in many cases is much more comforting and reassuring. Finally, I will talk about the societal stigma that often accompanies epilepsy.

••• **Fast Fact** •••
About 60 million people around the world have epilepsy.

A Brief History of Epilepsy

The Distant Past

Accounts of epilepsy date back thousands of years before the Common Era. Indeed, there exists a Babylonian tablet, dating from around 2000 BCE, that actually records various seizure types. At that time, however, epilepsy was understood only as a spiritual condition, which had to be dealt with through religion.

In 400 BCE, Hippocrates wrote the first book on the subject of epilepsy, *On the Sacred Disease*, in which he debunked the common belief that epilepsy was a form of supernatural condition. He explained that it was caused by naturally occurring disorders in the brain, not by curses or prophesies. Epilepsy was also mentioned in biblical times, and the Bible itself refers to the symptoms of epilepsy in the gospel of Mark.

In some early societies, people with epilepsy were considered to be under the influence of the changing phases of the moon. This led to the term *lunatic*, which in Latin means moonstruck, or crazy. It was common for people with epilepsy to be outcasts from society, and they were frequently punished. Even so, over time many people with epilepsy have risen to great heights despite their condition.

Who Gets Epilepsy?

Among all people with epilepsy, the gender breakdown is 48 percent female and 52 percent male. There are two times in life when epilepsy is more likely to occur: during childhood and after the age of 55. In the United States, about 9 out of every 1,000 people are treated for epilepsy in any

> given year, and up to 5 percent of the world's population may have one or more seizures at some time in their lives.

In colonial America, a person having a seizure was thought by some to have been overtaken by a demonic spirit. This superstition led to tragic events in Salem, Massachusetts, where, in the late 1600s, young girls would simulate seizures as part of their "proof" that certain women in the town were witches casting spells on children. And sadly, at that time and place any woman who happened to have seizures was branded as a handmaiden of the devil.

Advances during the Last 200 Years

The latter half of the 19th century saw great strides in the understanding of epilepsy, when English neurologists more clearly defined the medical basis of the condition and identified how seizures can alter consciousness and behavior. These breakthroughs were followed in 1904 by the coining of the term *epileptologist* (pronounced ep-ill-ep-TAHL-ah-jist) to describe a neurologist who specializes in this disease.

A milestone in the history of epilepsy was reached in 1929, when a German psychiatrist, Hans Berger, invented a method of recording the electrical activity in a person's brain and printing it on a strip of paper. This technology, termed the *electroencephalogram (EEG)*, is still key to the diagnosis of epilepsy today.

Since 1940, many new drug discoveries have led to remarkable advances in the treatment of epilepsy. Of course, drug research continues to this day as scientists attempt to find new and better ways to help children and adults deal with the wide variety of epilepsies and seizure types.

In 1968, the Epilepsy Foundation of America was founded. Now called simply the Epilepsy Foundation, this group is dedicated to sharing information and promoting the health and wellbeing of people with epilepsy.

> ## Who Treats Epilepsy?
>
> As we have learned much more about epilepsy, treating the disease has become a specialty in its own right. In fact, there are several levels of involvement within the epilepsy universe, from family practice physicians, internists, and pediatricians to general and pediatric neurologists. And there are numerous people pursuing epilepsy subspecialties within neurology, with precise focuses on surgical therapy, drug therapy, and many other areas.
>
> Of course, excellent care for epileptic patients is provided every day at community hospitals across the United States. Those efforts can be supported by specialized epileptic centers that concentrate on specific areas of treatment, such as pediatric epilepsy or epilepsy surgery. Sometimes, to uncover the underlying causes of epilepsy, a patient must be referred to specialists. (Causes are addressed specifically in chapter 3.) In other cases, the cause may be known, but a specialist is needed to treat that particular type of epilepsy. I will discuss these issues later in the book.

One of the most important technological advances in the last few decades has been the development of *neuroimaging* equipment, especially *Magnetic Resonance Imaging (MRI)*. MRI can detect small brain lesions and other abnormalities, making possible the diagnosis of clearly specific epilepsies. This in turn opens the door for surgical intervention, when such an approach is appropriate.

A significant step forward was taken in 1990 when the Americans with Disabilities Act (ADA) was passed and signed into law. Before this law was enacted, some states had laws that did not allow people with epilepsy to marry or become parents. Shockingly, in some states it was possible to sterilize people with epilepsy without their consent! The ADA clearly prohibits discrimination on the basis of disability.

The Myths

Over the millennia, many myths about epilepsy and people who have epilepsy have arisen and, unfortunately, some myths persist.

Perhaps one reason is that an epileptic seizure, particularly a *grand mal seizure*, with involuntary jerking movements of the whole body, can look pretty scary. And since the average person is rarely, if ever, exposed to such an event, misconceptions can easily grow among an uninformed public.

Here are some common myths and the very different realities.

The Myth: People with Epilepsy Are Crazy or Possessed

The reality: Epilepsy is a physical, functional problem that happens to occur in the brain. An epileptic seizure is an unprovoked and unpredictable interruption of a person's daily life that can cause problems for the person experiencing it and those witnessing it. The fearful response to this physical disorder stems from the disorientation of witnesses who are unfamiliar with the sight of someone in the throes of a seizure.

Unlike the symptoms of most diseases, epileptic seizures imbue the patient with an otherworldly appearance, as if his body had been invaded by an unnatural force. Even though he's unconscious during the seizure, he does not look like someone at peace. These factors feed the imaginations of witnesses and lead to highly erroneous conclusions.

The stigma of epilepsy endures today, even though we know much more about it and how to treat it than we did in decades and centuries past. As a result, few public figures such as actors, politicians, or other celebrities have stepped forward and admitted they have epilepsy. This is in notable contrast to the famous people with other diseases, such as AIDS and Parkinson's, who have been open about their conditions, and in some cases become spokespersons for their diseases.

We can only hope that this stigma will lessen over time as people learn more about epilepsy and its true nature. And on a personal note, I hope this book will make a contribution to that effort.

The Myth: No Famous People Have Had Epilepsy

The reality: Over the expanse of recorded history, there have been many people with epilepsy who have achieved great things in virtually all fields. A short list of these individuals includes:

- Socrates, Greek philosopher

- Alexander the Great, Greek general and statesman

- Julius Caesar, Roman statesman

- Napoleon, French emperor

- Lord Byron, English poet

- Fyodor Dostoyevsky, Russian novelist

- Vincent van Gogh, Dutch painter

- Alfred Nobel, Swedish munitions manufacturer, founder of the Nobel Prize

- Many, many more

One of the best known of all the world figures to have had epilepsy is Fyodor Dostoyevsky, the famous Russian writer. Unlike many others, Dostoyevsky never hid his epilepsy, and he used the condition as a theme in his novels. He gave several of his characters epilepsy, including Prince Myshkin, hero of *The Idiot*. Dostoyevsky described the effects of Myshkin's seizures with penetrating accuracy.

The Myth: People with Epilepsy Aren't as Smart as the Average Person

The reality: While the intelligence of the entire population of people with epilepsy is statistically slightly lower than the average, intelligence is a highly individual phenomenon. As noted earlier, there have been quite a few geniuses among people with epilepsy.

Epilepsy itself generally has little or no effect on a person's ability to think, except during those brief moments when a seizure is taking place. Because epilepsy drugs act on the brain, physicians must be vigilant in ascertaining that drugs aren't having a negative effect on learning, alertness, or functioning.

The Myth: People Who Have Seizures Can't Handle High-Pressure, Highly Demanding Jobs

The reality: They often can . . . and they do.

Of course, there are some jobs that people with epilepsy should not pursue, such as a jet fighter pilot or a scuba diver. And some individuals are more affected by the stresses caused by certain jobs, such as the sleep deprivation faced by long-haul truckers, which can lower the threshold for seizures. But most professions can accommodate a person with epilepsy with little or no trouble.

There are countless people with epilepsy who work in the highest tiers of business, government, medicine, and virtually all walks of life. Because epilepsy is experienced so individually, each person must judge for herself the kinds of work she wants to do and is capable of doing.

The Myth: People with Epilepsy Appear Different—You Can Spot Such a Person on Sight

The reality: There is no physical manifestation of epilepsy outside the seizure itself. If other features are present, such as motor or learning problems, they're due to the underlying cause and not the epilepsy.

The Myth: Epilepsy Is Often Accompanied by Other Physical Ailments, Handicaps, and Disabilities

The reality: While epilepsy can occur along with other physical or mental problems, it often stands alone as the only significant medical issue a person has to confront. There is not necessarily an inevitable slide into other problems once epileptic seizures are diagnosed.

The Myth: Epilepsy Is Contagious

The reality: No, it isn't. Enough said.

The Myth: Epilepsy Can't Be Caused by an Event that Happened a Long Time before the First Seizure Ever Occurred

The reality: Actually, some epilepsies can develop slowly over time, in reaction to a trauma, illness, or some other occurrence much earlier in life.

The Myth: It's Possible to Predict Seizures If You Just Try Hard Enough

The reality: Unfortunately, no, it isn't. But research is active in this area, and we hope that someday it will be possible to help a patient know when a seizure is coming on.

In the meantime, some dogs are being trained to use their heightened senses to actually predict when a person's seizure is about to occur. The dogs signal a warning by various means that allows time for that person or others nearby to take precautions to ensure that no harm is done when the seizure arrives. Although this is a promising area of epilepsy prediction, there are no guarantees that any particular dog will be able to provide this service. So be very wary of claims made by dog trainers who may sell such a pooch under false pretenses.

The Myth: Seizures Hurt

The reality: Watching a friend or loved one experience a grand mal seizure is difficult, but remember that this person is unconscious and not in pain. After a seizure, a person may feel some discomfort resulting from muscle aches or stiffness, a bitten tongue, bruises from a fall, burns from contact with a stove or other heat source, or other scratches and scrapes. (See "Take Action: Responding to a Generalized Tonic-Clonic Seizure," chapter 2.)

The Myth: During a Seizure, a Person Is Likely to Swallow His Tongue

The reality: It's not possible. This misunderstanding can cause a serious problem if witnesses try to put something into an epileptic person's mouth during a seizure in a misguided attempt to prevent that person from swallowing his tongue. Such an action can cause serious damage to teeth and gums, or it can cause breathing difficulties. In fact, you might even be bitten while contributing nothing to the person's safety or well-being.

However, a person might sometimes bite his tongue or the inside of his cheeks during the seizure, causing soreness in those areas. These minor bite wounds heal quickly and aren't a major concern beyond the discomfort they cause.

The Myth: Epilepsy Cannot Be Effectively Controlled

The reality: As seen in all the evidence presented in this book, there are many ways to treat, minimize, control, and even eliminate epilepsy when the conditions are right.

While there are some people whose epilepsy is so serious that the seizures just cannot be controlled, this group is becoming smaller as new treatments and medications are developed.

Also, the side effects from medications have become better appreciated, and we can use that knowledge to significantly improve the quality of life for most people with epilepsy.

What You Should Know

- Epilepsy is a physical, functional problem that happens to occur in the brain.

- Although epilepsy has been with us since antiquity, great strides in diagnosis and treatment have been made in the last 100 years.

- There are many ways to treat, minimize, control, and even eliminate epilepsy when the conditions are right.

- People with epilepsy may be smart, famous, and highly productive, just like anyone else.

Chapter 2

Epilepsy Is a Physical Disorder, Not a Mental Disease

Contrary to popular opinion, epilepsy is not a mental illness but a physical problem that happens to occur in the brain and that affects the nervous system.

Now and then, nerve cells in the brain of an epilepsy patient send out excessive electrical impulses—a sort of electrical storm in the brain. These neurological disturbances cause episodes that are called seizures. Seizures can range from an odd sensation in the stomach and a vague feeling of confusion to whole-body stiffness and jerky motions.

When a seizure is suspected, it's important that a physician be contacted, as you will see from Cassie's story.

Cassie

When Cassie woke up in the ambulance, she had no idea where she was or why she was there. The last thing she remembered was getting ready for her presentation to Lander Industries regarding its new marketing campaign. As a personable and ambitious junior account executive with C. Bryan Advertising, Cassie was eager to show her grasp of her client's business as well as to describe her firm's exciting advertising ideas.

At age 24, Cassie was working under the watchful eye of Jake, a senior account manager. He was giving her a chance to take the lead in this meeting, and she appreciated it.

With this new responsibility in her mind, she had spent the previous night running through the presentation as she tossed and turned in her bed. Now here she was, staring up at the wires, tubes, and blinking lights inside the ambulance. Thinking back, all she could recall was a strange feeling in her stomach as she had been waiting in the agency conference room for the client to arrive. Just butterflies, *she had thought at the time.*

Cassie wasn't aware of the fact that back in the conference room her face had assumed a glazed look—a look that Jake noticed, along with her inability to respond to his gentle joshing about the presentation to come. Then she had begun smacking her lips and making fumbling motions with her fingers. Just as Jake became concerned, Cassie's body stiffened and she fell to the floor. Her legs and arms began to jerk as her complexion turned dusky and saliva appeared at the corners of her mouth.

Cassie's jerking lasted only a few minutes, but it seemed much longer for Jake and two other agency employees who walked past the conference room and saw what was happening. Not sure how to help her, they knelt and tried to make sure that as she flailed, she didn't hurt herself by hitting her arms and legs on anything solid. Afterward, when the emergency medical service ambulance arrived to take her to the hospital, Cassie was hard to rouse and pretty much out of it.

In the ER, Cassie was glad to see that her fiancé, Dan, had arrived, but she had a bad headache and was bone-tired. In my office, about 20 minutes later, she was getting back to normal. This indicated that there was probably no underlying acute or dangerous condition causing the seizure.

I had already contacted one of her coworkers and received the details of her seizure event, and based on the description of the attack, it seemed as if this were probably a first epileptic seizure. We then planned to have two tests performed: an electroencephalogram, known as an EEG, and a magnetic resonance imaging scan, known as an MRI.

The tests confirmed that Cassie had experienced an epileptic seizure. With the diagnosis confirmed, we discussed the pros and cons of beginning drug treatments. Cassie decided that she wanted to be protected as much as possible against future seizures, so medication was started, and she was able to return to her job and life.

Finding Your Way around the Brain

If you experience a seizure, the first things your doctor will want to discover include: Was the event an epileptic seizure? If so, was the seizure focal or generalized?

A *focal seizure* is limited to a specific segment of the brain. A *generalized seizure* happens all over the brain at the same time.

Determining the type of seizure is important because it is the first step in directing further diagnostic testing and treatment.

The seizures themselves provide clues to this distinction. To understand these clues, first we have to understand the geography of the brain.

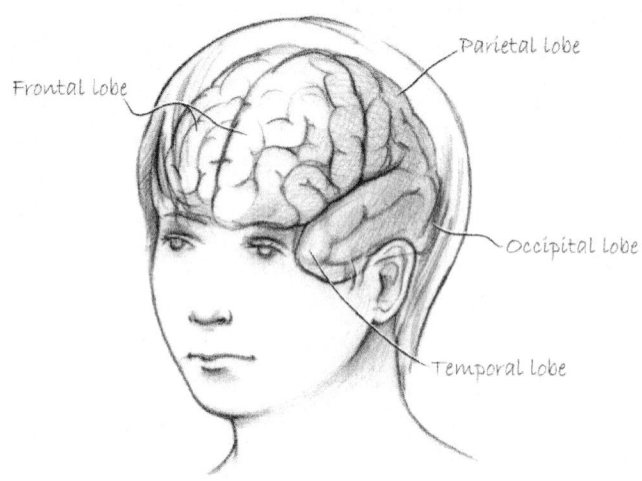

Figure 2.1. *Lobes of the brain.*

Frontal lobe: The *frontal lobe* is an area around the forehead that controls emotion, movement, reasoning and planning, and parts of speech. It also is involved in creativity.

Temporal lobes: Located just above the ears on both sides, the *temporal lobes* function in the areas of hearing, memory, and language. Temporal lobes process auditory information, turning sounds into meaning.

Language function is usually located in the frontal and temporal lobes on the left side of the brain, and motor functions for each side of the body are controlled by the frontal lobe on the opposite side of the brain. That is, the right side of the brain controls motor functions on the left side of the body; the left side of the brain controls motor functions on the right side of the body.

Parietal lobe: Behind the frontal lobe, the *parietal lobe* processes nerve impulses related to body sensations and is also involved in some language and thought functions.

Occipital lobe: Set in the back of the brain, the *occipital lobe* processes visual stimuli, allowing a person to recognize objects.

Types of Seizures

As discussed above, seizures can be focal or generalized.

A focal seizure affects only a particular segment of the brain, and as a result, displays symptoms that affect only the part of the body controlled by that area of the brain. Focal seizures may spread to involve other parts of the brain. In children, 50 to 60 percent of all seizures are focal or unclassified (many unclassified seizures ultimately turn out to be focal, which is why these two types are usually grouped together). For adults, roughly 90 percent of seizures are focal or unclassified.

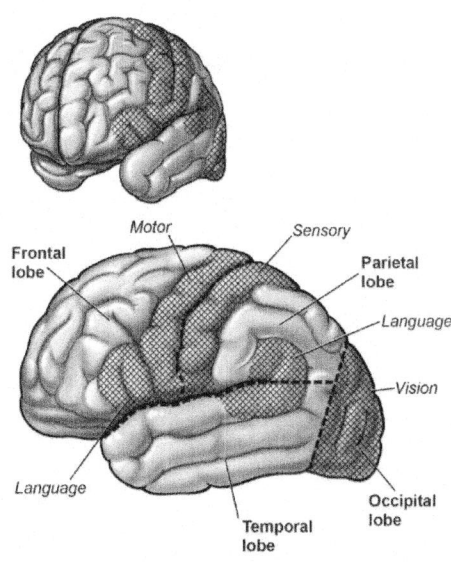

Figure 2.2. *Side (lateral) view of the left side of the brain, showing lobes and function.*

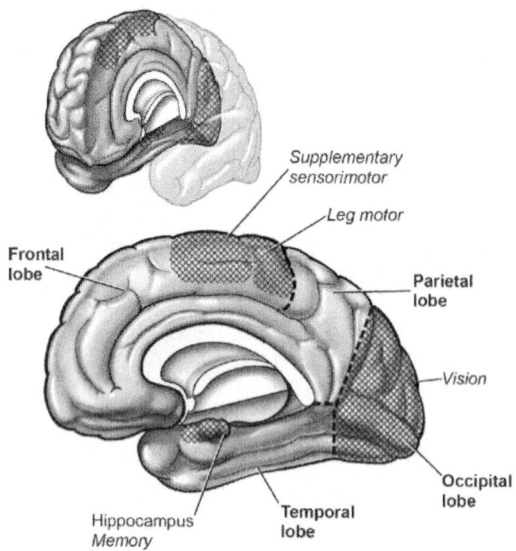

Figure 2.3. *View showing the lobes and functions on the right inside surface of the brain.*

A generalized seizure involves the whole brain.

Focal Seizures

Focal seizures fall into three main types:

1. **Aura**. An *aura* is a focal seizure involving sensation (any of the five senses) or perceptions, without the loss of consciousness.

2. **Complex partial seizure**. A *complex partial seizure* is a type of focal seizure involving the loss of consciousness.

Other terms for this form of epilepsy include *psychomotor* or *automotor seizures*.

3. Focal motor seizure. A *focal motor seizure* is a focal seizure that involves muscular motions.

Aura

This is the mildest kind of seizure. An aura occurs in a localized area of the brain. There is no loss of consciousness, but it causes disturbances to one or more senses or parts of the body.

Sometimes an aura can precede one of the other kinds of seizures (such as complex partial seizures), or it may exist by itself. Usually, an aura is a warning sign that another type of seizure is about to follow.

The range of auras includes:

- **Auditory aura (hearing)**. Often indicated by ringing, booming, buzzing, or machinelike sounds

- **Olfactory aura (smell)**. Usually an unpleasant odor such as burning rubber or sulfur, although some olfactory auras can be pleasant aromas

- **Gustatory aura (taste)**. Often with sharp, bitter, or sickly sweet tastes

- **Visual aura (vision)**. With spots, stars, blobs, bars, or circles of light—all one color or variously colored, stationary or moving

- **Psychic aura**. Can include difficulty in coordinating speech (dysphasia), distortion of memory or time sense, detachment, extreme pleasure or displeasure, and illusions or hallucinations

> ### Take Action
>
> The person experiencing an aura, or anyone who even suspects having had a mild seizure, should write down all the feelings and sensations that occurred at that time. This will help the doctor pinpoint the type of aura it was and may even provide clues to the location in the brain where the seizure began. For example, visual auras suggest a source in the occipital lobe, while an aura of tingling in the right hand suggests an onset in the left parietal lobe.

- **Epigastric (abdominal) aura**. A feeling of nausea, an unusual "rising" sensation, butterflies in the stomach, gastric tightness, or churning

- **Autonomic aura**. Includes disturbances to body functions not under conscious control, such as heartbeat, breathing, sweating, and sensory signals from muscles, joints, and skin

- **Vertiginous aura (dizziness)**. Characterized by feelings of displacement or movement, or a sensation of rotating

- **Somatosensory aura**. With tingling, numbness, an electrical feeling

- **Emotional aura**. Indicated by feelings (ranging from mild anxiety to intense terror) that are out of proportion to the situation

- **Sexual aura**. With erotic feelings sometimes accompanied by genital sensations

Complex Partial Seizures (with Impaired Consciousness)

This type of seizure usually arises in the temporal lobe. It may be accompanied by an aura, especially an abdominal or psychic aura. The aura may last anywhere from a few seconds up to a minute or two before consciousness is impaired.

Sometimes, a person experiencing a complex partial seizure can continue to interact with the environment to some extent for the duration of the seizure, but typically this ability is impaired. Afterward, the person may have no memory of the events that took place. The duration of the seizure is usually two to three minutes, but it may be as short as 30 seconds or as long as five to ten minutes—sometimes even longer.

Symptoms of complex partial seizures include:

- **Unresponsiveness**. An inability to respond to external stimuli, such as spoken words, visual gestures, and touch.

- **Automatic or unconscious actions (*automatisms*)**. These can include repetitive movements of the mouth and swallowing; repetitive hand movements and fumbling gestures; rapid eye-blinking; bicycling or pedaling movements of the legs; extreme facial expressions, grimacing, or pouting; or inappropriate laughter.

- **Stiffening or unnatural positioning (posturing) of the body, the arms, or the legs**.

- **Language disturbances**. These can include vocalizations such as moaning, whistling, or humming; or speech involving clearly understandable words (either repetitive or nonrepetitive, sensible or nonsensical).

- **Body disturbances**. These can include pallor, increased blood pressure, increased heartbeat, goose bumps, excess secretion of tears, dilated pupils, or vomiting.

- **Amnesia**. Whereby people experiencing impaired consciousness during seizures may be unaware of it afterward and unable to recall activities that occurred during or shortly after the seizure.

Take Action

If you're a witness to a complex partial seizure, try to take note of as many of the symptoms as possible to facilitate a quick and accurate diagnosis. Do not attempt to restrain the individual, but make safety the primary objective. Since judgment is impaired, move the person having a seizure away from danger—a stove, a staircase, an open window, a ladder—but do not try to restrain her. She may not be able to correctly interpret your actions, so remain low-key and nonintrusive.

Complex partial seizures may evolve to encompass other areas of the brain and body.

Focal Motor Seizures

Focal motor seizures begin in the central region of the brain, in the region where the frontal lobe meets the parietal lobe.

Symptoms of focal motor seizures include:

- **Stiffening, jerking, or twitching of muscles in a particular area of the body**. Typically, if there's an aura before a focal motor seizure, it's also localized. For example, a person might experience a tingling or numbness in his hand, followed by the hand jerking. Or he might feel tingling or numbness in the face, followed by facial twitching.

- **Minor but persistent twitching of a finger or a more vigorous muscle disturbance that is limited in duration to a few minutes**. If strong movement occurs in one particular part of the body, the seizure may be followed by weakness or temporary paralysis in that area. This is known as *Todd's paralysis*. This condition usually abates within 48 hours.

A focal motor seizure may evolve into other areas of the brain and body, becoming a full-blown convulsion, or it may remain localized. There are several special types of focal motor seizures.

Special Types of Focal Motor Seizures

Supplementary sensorimotor seizures. A supplementary sensorimotor area is located on each of the frontal lobes, on each side of the brain. Here, the brain can control both sides of the body from either side of the brain (in contrast with other motor areas, in which the right side of the brain controls the left side of the body, and vice versa). These areas of the brain put it all together and allow us to coordinate the motions of all our limbs simultaneously.

Supplementary sensorimotor seizure symptoms include big, thrashing movements involving all four limbs. Even though several parts of the body are affected, in terms of the brain, the seizure is still focal, or localized. Since either side of the brain can cause this activity, it isn't always readily apparent on which side the seizure is located. Usually these "hypermotor" seizures happen during sleep.

Versive seizures. In medical language, *version* means the turning of a part of the body from its natural position.

Versive seizures start near certain regions of the frontal or occipital lobes that control head and eye movements. The seizure can also evolve into other areas of the brain, affecting other parts of the body.

Versive seizure symptoms may include an unnatural turning of the head and eyes to one side. This may be the only manifestation, or it may be accompanied by other symptoms, such as loss of consciousness, the body jerking on the same side, and facial twitching. The side to which the head turns can indicate which side of the brain is experiencing the seizure.

Finding the Right Doctor

Often, your internist, family practice physician, or pediatrician will be well versed in epilepsy and can offer the information and guidance you need. But you may want to ask whether it would be appropriate for you to see a neurologist right from the start. You can make this decision yourself if you would feel more comfortable consulting with a specialist from the beginning.

There are different levels of treatment for epilepsy, up to and including dedicated epilepsy centers staffed with specialists, such as neurologists specializing in epilepsy. You should try to determine the right path of treatment based on all the relevant factors in your life (such as where you live, your ability to travel to find specialized care, and other circumstances).

Questions for Your Doctor
Your doctor is likely to ask for and offer considerable information about your seizure. But if the physician doesn't bring up these issues, there are

some things you can ask about, such as:

- Are you sure it was a seizure? Is there anything else it could have been?
- Are any additional tests required to clarify the situation?
- How shall I handle the next seizure? Under what conditions should I call for an ambulance?
- Are there emergency numbers I can call if I need help at night or on weekends?
- Do I need to see a specialist now?
- Can you recommend any specialists in this community?
- What can I expect in the future? How will my life change?
- Will any new problems emerge?
- Will this problem go away, or will it be with me for a long time?
- What are the potential risks and benefits of any suggested therapies?

After the first seizure, it may not be possible for your physician to fully answer some of these questions. But these are some of the issues you should be aware of and discuss over time, when it's appropriate.

Generalized Seizures

Generalized seizures involve the entire brain, so when muscle movements are involved, they're usually not limited to one side of the body.

Generalized Tonic-Clonic Seizures (Grand Mal)

A *generalized tonic-clonic seizure* is the type of seizure many people think of when they hear the word *epilepsy*. Marked by a loss of consciousness and stiffening and/or jerking of the muscles throughout the body, including arms and legs, these seizures are often referred to as grand mal seizures (it means "great ailment" in French).

Any of the focal seizures described on pages 22 to 23 can evolve into generalized tonic-clonic seizures. The term *tonic-clonic* refers to certain kinds of body movements that appear during the seizures. *Tonic* means sudden stiffening of the limbs; *clonic* refers to rhythmic jerking.

Primary and Secondary Generalized Tonic-Clonic Seizures

A *primary generalized seizure* starts all over the brain at the same time. It begins with sudden stiffening, perhaps an unnatural vocalization, a fall, or jerking all over. There's no warning (aura) or focal motor component; it just occurs out of the blue. Often, the skin takes on a dusky appearance, saliva foams at the mouth, the lips are bloody from tongue-biting, and there can be involuntary urination. The seizures usually last one to three minutes, but can last longer. Sometimes the stiffening occurs without the jerking, or the jerking happens with little or no stiffening.

Secondary generalized seizures result from the spread of the electrical storm from a localized trigger zone to all parts of the brain.

After a generalized tonic-clonic seizure has concluded, the patient may breathe deeply initially while his normal respiration returns. Often, the person falls asleep and awakens feeling tired, complaining of muscle aches and a headache.

The seizure itself usually lasts only a few minutes, but the postictal period (after the convulsion) may last from 15 minutes to a few hours. For this reason it's sometimes difficult to determine the exact duration of the seizure. Complete reorientation to the environment usually happens within 20 minutes. The individual may have a sore mouth if the tongue or cheek was bitten during the seizure.

Take Action: Responding to a Generalized Tonic-Clonic Seizure

If you're present when someone is having a generalized tonic-clonic seizure, here are steps you can take to enhance her safety:

1. Cushion her head, remove her glasses, and loosen any tight clothing that may constrict her movements.
2. Do not attempt to place an object in her mouth to immobilize her open jaw at the beginning of a seizure. Since the mouth closes so quickly at the onset of a seizure, trying to insert an object may cause more damage than the seizure itself would produce.
3. Try to turn her on her side to avoid aspiration (inhalation) of mouth contents. Speak calmly and, if others are present, quietly explain that she's having a seizure.
4. Remember, there's no way to make the seizure end faster, so shaking her or yelling at her won't help.
5. When the seizure comes to an end, she may have a headache and may want to sleep it off. Sleep will cause no harm, so there's no need to try to keep her awake. If or when she's awake, be sure that she's fully conscious and aware before you leave her on her own. You can do this by making sure she knows the date, where she is, and where she's going next.
6. Confusion may last longer than the seizure, and it can lead to dangerous behavior. If she wants to walk around, walk with her and make sure she's safe. It will help later if you can time the duration of the seizure.
7. Most seizures in people with epilepsy are not medical emergencies and do not require an ambulance or trip to the emergency room. However, it's a good idea to call an ambulance in any of the following situations:
   - Full awareness does not return.
   - You know the patient does not have epilepsy, or she has no epilepsy or seizure-disorder identification.
   - The seizure lasts more than five minutes.
   - There's a slow recovery, a second seizure, or difficulty breathing after the seizure ends.

> • She's pregnant or has another medical diagnosis.
> • There are any signs of injury or sickness.
>
> If the seizure appears to last longer than five minutes, you should call an emergency medical service, since professional intervention or rescue medications may be required. Rescue medications are available for emergency use at home, school, or other locations if prolonged seizures are recurrent.
>
> The first generalized tonic-clonic seizure is a serious event, and I urge prompt attention by a physician so that the condition can be diagnosed and treated. This will help minimize any adverse impact on the patient.

Myoclonic Seizures

Characterized by sporadic muscle jerks (as compared to the rhythmic jerking in clonic or tonic-clonic seizures), *myoclonic seizures* frequently involve the head, trunk, and limbs, and feature sudden, brief muscle contractions, either isolated or in small clusters. Sometimes these seizures are powerful enough to cause a person to tilt forward or backward and fall, and they usually occur without a detectable loss of consciousness.

Myoclonic muscle jerks that occur during seizures are similar to but usually stronger than the normal jerks that awaken you just as you're about to fall asleep.

Atonic Seizures

Atonic seizures, also called drop attacks or akinetic seizures, are characterized by a sudden loss of general muscle tone that occurs without any warning. The visual signs are a nodding head or slumping posture. Sometimes an intense loss of tone can cause an immediate fall or drop straight downward. (This movement gave rise to the phrase "the falling sickness" as a synonym for epilepsy.)

Epileptic Spasms

Epileptic spasms occur most often in infants, and in these cases, they're known as *infantile spasms*. The spasms tend to appear in clusters for several minutes, especially during the transition into or out of sleep.

Symptoms of epileptic spasms include:

- **Flexing or extending**. This can happen with the trunk, arms, and legs.

- **Bending forward**. The arms and legs are extended in the classic diver's posture.

- **Eye deviation**. This can include looking up or to the right or left unnaturally.

- **A combination of the symptoms listed above**.

Absence Seizures (Epileptic Staring Spells)

Most common in school-age children, *absence seizures* usually last ten seconds or so and may occur several times a day. They're commonly referred to as *petit mal seizures*. (Pronounced "petty mall," it means "small ailment" in French.) Sometimes children with absence seizures will also have generalized tonic-clonic seizures.

Symptoms of absence seizures include:

- **A fixed, blank stare**. The eyes may roll upward briefly while the person is motionless.

- **Mild muscle twitches**. These may involve the eyelids, corners of the mouth, fingers, or arms.

- **A sudden slight forward slump of head or trunk**. Muscles in face or jaw may slacken. The person may drop anything held in the hands.

- **Minor stiffening movements of the head or trunk**.

- **Automatic movements (automatisms)**. These include licking and swallowing, fiddling and scratching.

Absence seizures have an abrupt onset and stop equally quickly, with an elapsed time of seconds rather than minutes. The seizures typically occur daily and are not accompanied by an aura.

Clearly, it can be difficult to tell the difference between a focal and a generalized staring spell. EEG testing can be very helpful in making this diagnosis.

Atypical absence seizures. The term *atypical absence seizure* is used to describe epileptic staring spells accompanied by additional symptoms. Compared with typical absence seizures, atypical ones may last longer, may come and go with less clearly defined beginnings and endings, and may include more frequent but subtle motor symptoms, such as head nodding and slumping.

Take Action

Sometimes it's hard to distinguish between an absence seizure and a child's ordinary inattention or daydreaming. Watch for these four signs that the event may be an absence seizure:

1. The child's staring often interrupts play or other activities.

2. The staring child isn't responsive to touch or other external stimuli.

3. The staring occurs not only when the child is bored or in the stressful setting of a classroom, but at other times as well.

4. The staring is accompanied by some of the unnatural symptoms described above, such as muscle twitching, head nodding, or upward eye rolling.

Because staring and unresponsiveness are typical features of both absence seizures and complex partial seizures, diagnosis is made using EEG testing to distinguish between the two syndromes. Proper diagnosis has important implications for treatment.

Febrile seizures. Brought on by fevers in infants and small children, *febrile seizures* are most often characterized by loss of consciousness and shaking or moving limbs on both sides of the body. Children who have febrile seizures are not considered to have epilepsy, since epilepsy is defined as two or more seizures that are not directly triggered by a fever or other provocation. Medication is usually not required, and the child outgrows the tendency for such seizures by age five or six.

Take Action: Responding to a First Seizure

If you think you or a loved one may have had a seizure, here's what you should do.

If you have a serious seizure and there are witnesses, as happened with Cassie, the problem may be rather obvious. However, if you find yourself alone when the seizure happened, you may know from past experience that something unusual has occurred. Or there may be clues that you momentarily lost consciousness (such as missing an exit on a freeway or getting into a fender-bender), in which case you should consider whether something similar has happened before. If you suspect that you've had a seizure, it's best to see a doctor and explore the situation further. Take the following steps:

1. Call your physician or go to an emergency room.

2. Try to remember everything you can about the seizure and write it all down. How did it start? Was only one side of your body affected? Which side? How long did the seizure last? Were there any other symptoms? Has this or something similar happened before? The more you can tell the doctor, the better the diagnosis can proceed. Remember to bring any medications you may be taking.

3. Start taking precautions:

    - Do not go swimming or take a bath without someone present to help in case of a seizure. There's a definite risk of drowning if a person experiences a seizure while taking a bath. Showers are recommended.

    - A person with epilepsy should put temperature controls on the faucets of the bathtub and sinks to avoid scalding if a seizure should occur.

    - A person who has experienced one seizure should not drive for at least six months. Before driving is resumed, the physician must be certain that the seizure will not recur or that a proper treatment protocol is being followed. (Chapter 10 will address this issue in more detail.)

    - Be sure that the individual wears a helmet when riding a bicycle. (A good idea for everyone, by the way!)

    - Use common sense about climbing ladders or scaling heights, operating heavy machinery, and so on.

Recurrence of Seizures

After a first seizure, it's important to understand that there may be other episodes. In some scenarios, it may be best to wait and see whether there's another seizure before starting daily medication. The physician is the best person to recommend that course of action. The risk is significantly higher for recurrence if the EEG or MRI shows abnormality or if there exists other neurological impairment or a previous brain injury.

In the case of an initial and uncomplicated grand mal seizure, the chances of recurrence are in the range of 30 percent. Even though that represents a higher likelihood of seizure than for people who have never experienced one, the odds are still fairly good that you won't have a recurrence.

When seizure recurrences do take place, 50 percent occur within six months of the initial seizure and 80 percent within two years. Late recurrences are unusual, but they have been documented up to ten years after the initial event.

If a second seizure occurs, the chances for further recurrences increase significantly, to about 80 percent.

Status Epilepticus: The Most Serious Type of Seizure

Occurring at first onset or as part of chronic epilepsy, *status epilepticus* is a phenomenon in which a person goes into a long, life-threatening seizure or a series of seizures. This event requires immediate emergency care and specialized drugs, with stabilization in an intensive care unit.

Status epilepticus may result from various medical conditions such as encephalitis, meningitis, and other acute illnesses. It can also occur in people with chronic epilepsy who do not take their medication regularly. Regardless of its origin, it is always serious and must be dealt with immediately.

If you know that a person is prone to prolonged seizures, you should have the rescue medication on hand at all times (at school, at work—anywhere the patient is likely to be) and be sure that someone knows how to administer it. The drug should be administered immediately, without waiting for the seizure to evolve. Make sure the patient is wearing a medical alert necklace or carrying information that advises emergency room doctors of critical medical details.

What You Should Know

Seizures may be focal or generalized. The signs of a focal seizure depend on the part of the brain that is affected:

- **Frontal lobe**. Language, motor control

- **Parietal lobe**. Sensation, other intellectual functions

- **Temporal lobe**. Language, memory; where sound is transformed into meaning

- **Occipital lobe**. Translates visual stimuli into meaning
There are different types of focal seizures, including:

- **Aura**. Sensory disturbance with no loss of consciousness, sometimes preceding more serious seizures

- **Complex partial seizures**. Altered awareness, often with automatisms or other signs

- **Focal motor seizures**. Stiffening or jerking of a localized part of the body

Generalized seizures start all over the whole brain at one time. There are several types of generalized seizures, including:

- **Generalized tonic-clonic seizures**. Stiffening and jerking of the body and all four limbs

- **Myoclonic seizures**. Sporadic muscle jerks of the head, trunk, and limbs

- **Atonic seizures**. Sudden loss of muscle tone with head nodding, slumping posture, or fall

- **Epileptic spasms**. Clusters of spasms with flexing or extension of the trunk, arms, and legs

- **Absence seizures**. Staring and altered awareness

Status epilepticus is a prolonged generalized or focal seizure or cluster of seizures that requires emergency treatment.

Chapter 3

Diagnosing Epilepsy

Finding a Cause Can Be as Important as . . . Not Finding One

Whenever a person experiences the symptoms of an epileptic seizure, physicians want to know the cause. Often, the individual exhibiting the symptoms and the family aren't as concerned with the cause as they are with treatment. Understandably, they're focused on trying to avoid or to moderate such upsetting and potentially dangerous seizures. But determining the cause, if possible, is an enormously valuable step.

Sometimes the seizure is a sentinel event, pointing toward a serious underlying condition, such as a brain tumor or a stroke, which needs immediate attention. In some cases, the underlying cause may be correctable, and if it's found and fixed or controlled, the epilepsy may disappear. This can happen to people with hypoglycemia, diabetes, or disorders resulting from calcium or sodium imbalance in which the epilepsy occurs as a secondary phenomenon.

When an inherited genetic or metabolic problem causes epileptic seizures, there may be reproductive risks for the patient or for his siblings. Whether that problem can be addressed medically or not, it's important that the patient and any siblings be told of this causal condition so that they can make informed decisions about how they live their lives.

Even if none of the tests comes back positive, the physician can sometimes "ballpark" a diagnosis of the cause, basing his conclusion on a set of symptoms that are commonly found in a particular kind of epilepsy. As a result, the individual can be told that his particular epilepsy, such as *juvenile myoclonic epilepsy*, does not require genetic counseling or further testing, but will call for long-term medication.

Take Dan as an example.

Dan

Dan, an MD and renowned epileptologist, was proud to be speaking before a group of neurologists at Cleveland Clinic. In his years teaching and working at Harvard, Dan had carved out a reputation as an expert in epilepsy research. He was eager to share his insights with his peers at the Clinic, and he also wanted to learn what they could teach from their experiences.

With his well-developed and sneaky sense of humor, Dan enjoyed inserting a few puns into his speeches, especially when he knew that fellow doctors would pick up on his wordplay and banter. So the lecture had been both informative and entertaining. Dan was just about to launch into his concluding statements when he sensed the feeling he had described to others so many times before.

He realized that he was feeling strange. After a few seconds, he noticed that his head was jerking and turning toward his left side and that it wasn't under his control. Then he blacked out. Observers in the audience had seen Dan's head making ratcheting movements toward his left and that his face was pulling and jerking on the left side. His left arm was raised in a hitchhiking pose and was also jerking back and to the left. He then made a noise, stiffened, and collapsed to the floor.

Dan's grand mal convulsion lasted for a minute or two. Of course, the physicians in the auditorium, all specialists in neurology, rushed to his aid and made sure he was turned on his side and that his glasses were removed to avoid any injury. While they neither grabbed him nor held him down, they kept him safe and waited until the seizure passed before taking him into the hospital for testing.

When Dan awakened on a gurney in the hospital, he was groggy and confused, but soon he realized where he was and understood when he was told what had happened. An EEG performed that day showed sharp waves in the right frontal region of his brain, which helped pinpoint the problem. Later, an MRI showed a meningioma, which is a usually benign brain tumor that grows from the meninges, the fibrous casing around the brain. Although it is usually benign, as the tumor grows it can produce pressure on the brain that leads to abnormal electric impulses and irritations, which can manifest as a seizure.

Dan started taking medicines in order to avoid further seizures. After his return to Boston, he and his doctors decided to proceed with surgery to remove the tumor. Within weeks, the tumor was removed safely at his home hospital. He'll continue to take antiseizure medication, probably for a year or two, until physicians decide whether to continue drug therapy. In any case, his prognosis is extremely good.

The irony of Dan's seizure wasn't lost on him or his colleagues and friends. But the episode illustrates that an epileptic seizure can happen to anyone at any age, even to those of us who work in this field every day.

Diagnostic Tools

Once a person has experienced seizures and has consulted with a physician, the scheduling of neurological examinations is mandatory. These can include electroencephalogram examinations and magnetic resonance imaging scans.

Generally, patients presenting with seizures will receive an EEG test. If the physician looks at the EEG, considers the seizure symptoms, and thinks that the seizures are focal, he'll probably order an MRI. Since it's likely that something is wrong in a particular spot of the brain, an MRI can help identify malignant or benign brain tumors, a congenital brain malformation, injury from a previous stroke or trauma, and other anomalies. MRI tests are also useful in diagnosing causes of generalized seizures for some people.

The third level of testing is highly individualized and is based on the symptoms and the results of the EEG and MRI testing. A number of other procedures, including blood tests, genetic tests, and other lab work, will frequently help in pinpointing the cause.

In special cases, along with a complete medical history, other evaluations such as basic lab tests (blood and urine) and metabolic and genetic testing may be conducted, in the effort to uncover possible underlying causes resulting from preexisting medical conditions, drug reactions, and so forth. However, the gold standard for diagnosing epilepsy is the EEG.

Why an EEG Is So Important

The EEG machine translates the electrical activity of the brain into wavy lines on a computer screen or, in years past, on a scrolling sheet of paper. Electrodes attached to the scalp record tiny electrical charges, and any changes in the expected electrical activity are registered as spikes that disturb the flow of those wavy lines.

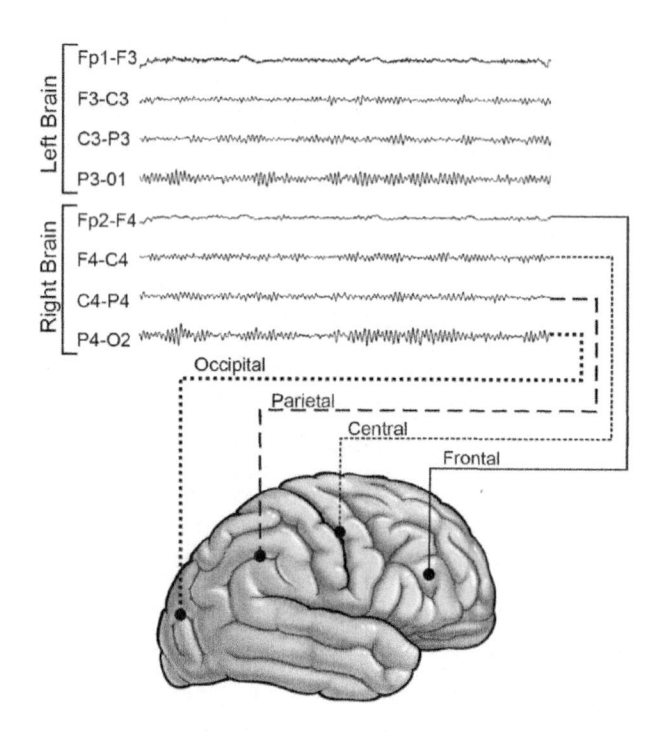

Figure **3.1**. *EEG showing ten seconds of normal electrical rhythms from both sides of the brain.*

An EEG is valuable for the following reasons:

- Even though the patient rarely has a seizure during a routine EEG test, the physician can recognize abnormal patterns in the wavy lines that indicate a risk for seizures.

- Depending on the particular pattern, the doctor can often determine whether all or part of the brain is being affected. This is key to developing a program of treatment, beginning with the first medication to be prescribed.

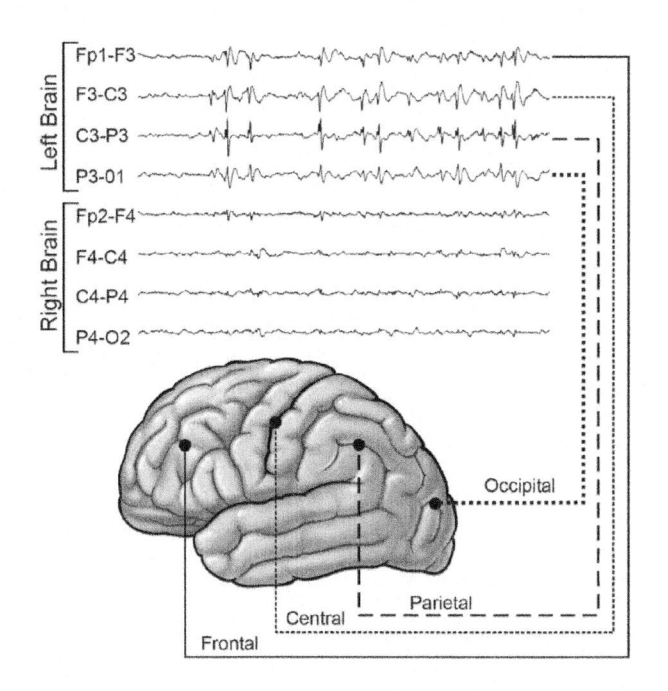

Figure 3.2. *EEG showing abnormal focal sharp waves on the left side of the brain. These discharges are interictal (seen during times when a seizure is not occurring) and did not awaken the child from sleep. Features of the discharges suggest benign focal epilepsy of childhood (see chapter 7).*

- The test may help to identify a specific type of epilepsy and may also predict how the epilepsy will evolve over time.

- The EEG test has a fundamental value in determining whether the patient is a future candidate for surgery in the event that the medications don't work.

- Finally, the EEG helps physicians arrive at a strategy for the operation, should it become necessary.

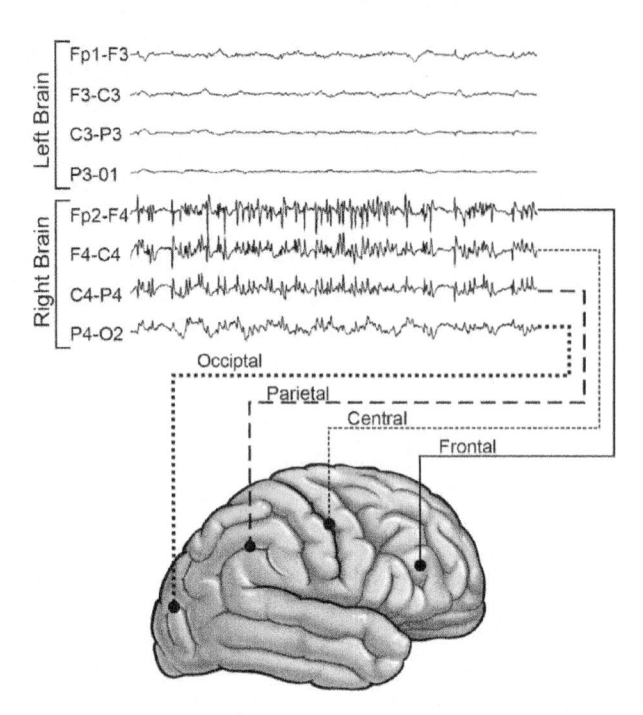

Figure 3.3. *EEG showing a focal seizure limited to the right side of the brain. During the seizure, the left arm and left side of the face jerked rhythmically for two minutes.*

The Advantages of an MRI

An MRI can be helpful for several reasons:

- Brain scans can help the physician initially determine whether the patient has suffered a stroke or has a tumor, brain malformation, or other underlying condition.

- Later on, scans can help greatly in identifying the site for possible surgical treatment if medication cannot control the epilepsy.

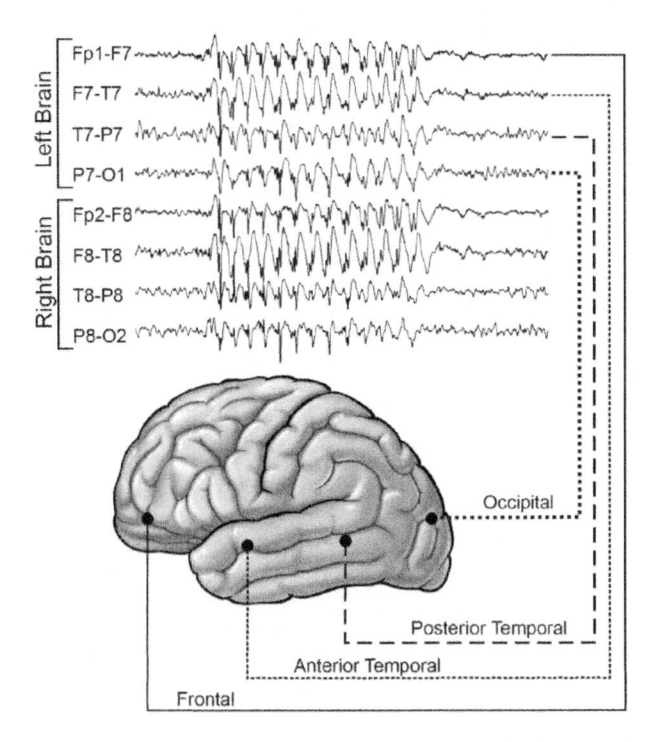

Figure 3.4. *EEG showing an abnormal seizure discharge lasting about five seconds in the middle of a ten-second period of recording. The discharge is generalized, seen on both sides of the brain. This pattern is typically seen in childhood absence epilepsy (see chapter 7, pages 104–105).*

While MRI scans can be extremely beneficial in revealing the underlying causes of epileptic seizures, other evaluations (such as metabolic and genetic testing, along with blood and urine testing) are necessary to develop a comprehensive picture of the patient's condition.

What Is an MRI Scan?

In the diagnosis of epilepsy, the MRI scan is an exciting area of testing, and thanks to this technology, new discoveries are being made.

An MRI uses a small amount of radio waves to excite subatomic elements of brain tissue, which then transmit energy back in a specific pattern as they relax and realign. This process is harmless, and the person undergoing the scan feels nothing. The MRI emissions are turned into a detailed picture of the brain that can be analyzed by the physician.

It's best to have an MRI performed on a state-of-the-art high-field scanner, so ask your doctor about the kind of equipment that is being used at the location where your tests will take place. Scans taken by low-field or open MRI equipment could miss subtle anomalies that could be causing a patient's seizures.

Usually, people with claustrophobia can tolerate the scanning process. If not, the doctor can provide a mild sedative to reduce an individual's anxiety and help the procedure go more smoothly. Since an MRI can last 40 minutes or more, with the patient remaining motionless during that time, infants and children must be sedated before the procedure.

Take Action

MRI testing enables the physician to confirm epilepsy diagnoses and detect anatomic lesions in the brain that might need treatment. That is why an MRI exam may be reasonable for almost every epilepsy patient to consider.

However, if your physician does not recommend an MRI, it may be that she recognizes a type of epilepsy in which the MRI scan is always normal. These types include such conditions as childhood absence epilepsy, juvenile myoclonic epilepsy, and benign focal epilepsy of childhood, as described later in chapter 7. Ask you doctor if this is the reason an MRI is not being requested.

Many times, no cause can be found . . . and that's often good news!

Types of Causes

A physician will always want to discover the root cause of epileptic seizures, but it often happens that no clear-cut cause is ever found. These cases, referred to by doctors as idiopathic, are often good news for the patient. When there's no obvious underlying cause for the seizures, a serious condition may not be present.

So while it may be a bit frustrating for everyone involved when a cause cannot be determined, it's wise to look on the bright side and recognize that idiopathic seizures often offer a more positive prognosis.

When a cause is found, it's either acute or remote:

- Acute causes are closely linked in time to the seizure and include such conditions as a recent stroke, trauma, chemical imbalance, and drug or alcohol abuse.

- Remote causes happen much earlier. The epilepsy develops over time, eventually resulting in a seizure when the person is significantly older. Examples of causes that may be remote are birth injury, brain malformations, and strokes that occurred some time ago.

Sometimes a patient's family wonders why the epilepsy is emerging so long after a brain injury.

For instance, in the case of birth trauma, motor impairments and learning problems are recognized almost immediately, but epilepsy may not appear until later. The reason for this delay is that epilepsy is related to the electric circuitry of the brain, and the abnormal circuitry that results in seizures often takes time to develop before the disease can be diagnosed accurately. This is true for both children and adults who experience brain trauma or other conditions mentioned above.

Neurological Causes of Epilepsy

Epilepsy may develop in response to a variety of brain injuries or abnormalities. The following are some of the most common neurological causes of epilepsy.

Tumors

Studies have shown that about 15 percent of people with epilepsy have a brain tumor. These tumors may be benign or malignant. Complete surgical removal of the tumor usually results in the cessation of seizures. If the tumor is malignant, radiation therapy may help decrease the number of seizures in individuals whose tumors cannot be entirely removed.

Stroke

Epilepsy can result from stroke at any stage of life. It can happen as a result of birth trauma, heart disease or heart surgery, hardening of the arteries, high blood pressure, and other conditions. But it's most frequently seen in infants and seniors.

Trauma

Head trauma is responsible for 5 percent of all epilepsy, and while most seizures occur in the first two years after a head injury, they may begin any time thereafter. Minor head trauma, such as a toddler falling out of a high chair, is rarely a cause.

However, penetrating head wounds or severe blunt trauma resulting in neurological problems or other post-injury symptoms (beyond what you might see with a concussion) can sometimes lead to epileptic seizures.

Hippocampal Sclerosis

Hippocampal sclerosis involves the loss of brain cells or neurons in the hippocampus, which is located in the inside region of the brain's temporal lobe, the area that affects memory functions.

This condition shows up on the MRI as a hippocampus that is smaller than normal and has a scarred appearance.

Brain Malformations

Since brain malformations occur during brain development prior to birth, they are present at birth. These malformations may lead to seizures immediately or at some time later in childhood.

Sometimes, genetic testing can help identify the cause of the malformation, but usually there's no known cause. Nonetheless, it's important to understand that the malformation was *not* caused by anything the mother did during pregnancy.

Genetic Abnormalities

There are approximately 200 inherited disorders that are known to cause epileptic seizures. This fact presents a challenge for physicians, who need to specifically identify the particular disorder in order to formulate the best treatment plan and provide appropriate family counseling. In many cases, doctors must observe their patients over time and conduct screening tests to find the underlying condition.

If a genetic cause is found, it may be possible to actually determine the defective gene. When a genetic cause is present, there may be important repercussions in terms of reproductive decisions for the individual as well as his family. There also may be special treatment issues with genetically based epilepsy.

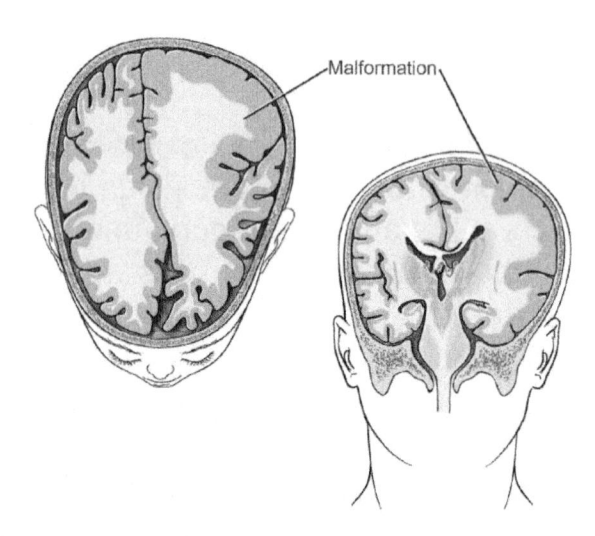

Figure 3.5. *Malformations of the brain may be localized in all or part of one hemisphere, as in this illustration, or they may involve both sides of the brain. This cause for seizures can be revealed by an MRI.*

Non-Neurological Conditions

Some seizures are caused by illnesses that do not occur in the brain or within the central nervous system. These conditions can include the following disorders:

- Imbalances in the blood chemistry: calcium, sugar (glucose), sodium, insulin

- Drug or alcohol abuse

- Infections

> ## Take Action
>
> You may be interested in obtaining a second opinion if you want to explore the issue of a possible underlying cause more fully or simply desire another perspective on your condition. Virtually all physicians will be happy to assist you in securing a second opinion. To do this, seek out 1 of the 50 comprehensive epilepsy centers in the United States. You want to find a physician who is board-certified in pediatric or adult neurology with a specialization in the treatment of epilepsy. You can ask your own doctor for a referral or seek assistance elsewhere. (For more information, see the appendix.)
>
> Information is also available through the websites of the National Association of Epilepsy Centers (*www.naecepilepsy.org*) and the Epilepsy Foundation (*www.epilepsyfoundation.org*).
>
> It's possible that you'll have to travel to see a specialist in seizure prevention and control, but if you do so, it may be time and money very well spent.
>
> Even if the information you gather through these efforts simply confirms the knowledge you already have, it will provide some peace of mind.

The key with non-neurological conditions is to diagnose and treat them directly, usually through blood and urine tests, to prevent further seizures.

Febrile Seizures

Fever-related seizures (*febrile seizures*) usually occur between six months and six years of age. Usually they're quite benign. Antiepileptic medications are usually not needed. It makes sense to try to control the fever, but such fevers and related seizures can be difficult to prevent. Once a pattern of febrile seizures is established, emergency treatment is usually not required—unless there's an underlying illness that requires medical attention.

Not All Seizures Are Epilepsy

There are a number of seizures that may seem to be epileptic convulsions but aren't. Some events, brought on by physical conditions such as *syncope* (pronounced SIN-ko-pe), cardiac irregularities, or arrhythmia, can involve falling or loss of consciousness, but are not epileptic seizures. If your physician is unsure, he may seek the help of a cardiologist to sort out the problem.

Events that arise from mental or emotional causes (the medical term is *psychogenic seizures*) may be misdiagnosed as epileptic seizures. Misdiagnosis can complicate treatment and multiply the problems for the patient, so psychiatric evaluation is important to make sure the diagnosis is accurate. As a general rule, when epilepsy isn't present, the routine interictal (between seizures) EEGs performed in brief office visits are always normal. A prolonged *video EEG* may be helpful to capture an actual episode and help determine what it is.

Take Action

Be aware that some seizures can fool you. If the episodes do not respond to treatment, it's important to look further into the situation. Be sure that the doctor has received all historical evidence regarding the person's seizures, along with a complete medical history. More testing, such as a video EEG or cardiac consultation, can help to clarify the issues and provide important clues as to whether the seizures are epileptic in nature. The doctor may need your help to get actual samples of previous EEGs done elsewhere or MRI films or discs for review.

If possible, try to record a seizure on home video equipment so that the physician can analyze the situation using firsthand evidence.

Take note that children especially may have a wide variety of episodic events (nonepileptic staring, tics, migraine headaches, and other phenomena) that may be confused with seizures.

What You Should Know

- It's important to determine the cause of epilepsy, especially because doing so will help your doctors to focus on the best treatment program.

- EEG is the gold standard for diagnosing epilepsy.

- MRI scans and other neuroimaging techniques can provide extremely detailed views of brain abnormalities.

- Sometimes finding no cause can actually be good news because it indicates no serious underlying condition.

Part Two

Treating Epilepsy

Chapter 4

Drug Therapy

The objective of epilepsy drug therapy is daily prevention of symptoms. Drugs won't cure the epilepsy. The epilepsy is still present, but medication can help suppress the symptoms so that the disease can be managed and the person can go on with his life.

Sometimes medication is started after the first seizure. In other cases, the doctor may recommend a wait-and-see approach before prescribing drug therapy. But usually, medication is indicated when epilepsy is present and seizures are recurring.

The next step is to determine the right drug or drug combination for each individual. Over the past several years, many new medications have become available, providing a wide array of choices and the opportunity for a physician to fine-tune the drug therapy for each person.

Janice's experience illustrates some of the issues that we must consider when we start treatment with an antiepileptic medication.

Janice

Twenty-eight-year-old Janice had never realized she would love motherhood so much before she gave birth to her son, Dwayne. But the three years that followed had been the happiest of her life. She treasured every moment as she watched her son grow and develop his own unique personality. Little Dwayne seemed to enjoy running into walls and falling off the couch, bouncing up and giggling every time, and Janice told her friends she thought she was raising either a stuntman or a daredevil. She and her husband, Lawrence, happily started planning to have another child.

But one day, while she was in the kitchen baking holiday cookies with a few friends, Janice fell and her arms and legs started jerking. She was having a brief seizure. Afterward, her friends took her to the emergency room. Although her EEG test and MRI were normal, from her friends' eyewitness reports and some evidence on examination that Janice had bitten her tongue and cheeks, I concluded that she had had an epileptic seizure, probably a grand mal convulsion.

After speaking with Janice and Lawrence in detail about her medical history and lifestyle, I decided that she should start taking medications. She needed to remain active and be able to drive, since her husband traveled frequently and she had to get around town on her own. But before I recommended a drug, I took into account that weight control was also an issue with Janice. That factor, in addition to the Davidsons' desire to have more children, shaped my decision as I chose a medication that would offer maximum safety in those areas. I also put her on a folic acid supplement for women who plan to become pregnant, as an added precaution against birth defects, as well as calcium and vitamin D to maximize long-term bone health.

Janice felt fine on the new drug, but about a month later she had another seizure. This happens sometimes, since it's difficult to establish precisely the right dose the first time. I adjusted the dose upward, and she seemed to tolerate it well initially. But a few days later, she felt slightly dizzy and a little unsteady on her feet, and she noticed some double vision. Upon hearing that, I immediately decreased the dosage to an amount midway between the first and the second dose. Janice has been doing beautifully ever since, without symptoms or side effects.

Then a few months later, I received an ecstatic call from her, announcing that she was pregnant again. After celebrating the good news, I told her that it would be important to monitor the level of medication in her bloodstream continually during her pregnancy because her condition would affect the way the drug would interact with her body. Doses often need to be increased during pregnancy. So we'd be seeing each other more often over the following months.

Nine months later, Janice gave birth to a healthy baby girl, and little Sondra gives no indication of wanting to pursue a career as a daredevil. At least not yet.

Janice's story indicates how important it is for a physician to use care in selecting the medications to be prescribed for epilepsy therapy, as well as how critical it is to monitor the effects and to adjust the dosages accordingly. When that is done, individuals with epilepsy can experience remarkable benefits from a program of medication.

Factors in the Process of Drug Selection

There are several factors physicians consider when selecting drugs for patients.

Will the Drug Be Effective?

This is the most important question to answer, and the physician will determine to the best of her ability which medications to select. Some drugs tend to be more effective for generalized epilepsies, while others have more positive effects on focal epilepsies. And some drugs, including many of the newer ones, produce good results for both conditions.

What Are the Potential Side Effects?

Every epilepsy drug has potential side effects. Some of these are dose-related, meaning that the side effects can often be eliminated by lowering the dose of the drug. Some common dose-related effects include fatigue, unsteadiness on your feet, and double vision.
Other side effects are rare, limited to certain susceptible individuals, and may not be dose-related. These effects tend to occur within the first six months of drug therapy, and they can be more serious. They include allergic hypersensitivity resulting in a mild or severe rash. Other effects can include injury to the liver and bone marrow.
Furthermore, every drug has its own particular range of side effects that may affect an individual. Your physician will determine which drugs are most effective for treating the specific epilepsy at hand and then prioritize them on the basis of the side effects that will least interrupt your lifestyle and have a minimum impact on your health profile. With some drugs, monitoring for side effects is suggested. Other drugs may not require any monitoring.
Among the factors a physician will consider in planning a drug therapy are the possible effects that drugs could have on:

- Weight gain or loss

- Long-term bone health

- Interactions with other drugs, such as birth control pills

- Attention and mood disorders

- Allergies to the drug

- Cost issues

There also may be greater or lesser concerns about the minor possibility of birth defects. Your physician will calibrate the drugs to find the optimum therapy after considering all these factors.

What about Bone Loss?

Recently, we became more aware that epilepsy and some of the drugs used to treat it can increase the risk of osteoporosis and result in reduced bone marrow density, as measured by specialized X-rays of the hip and spine. The risk increases with the length of time the drugs are taken and the number of drugs involved. Long-term use of some drugs can raise the risk of hip fracture by 400 percent and the chance of overall fractures by 200 percent, especially in seniors or in younger individuals who aren't able to engage in regular physical activity.

Since a person builds up bone mass early in life, whatever level an individual establishes by about the age of 20 is the level from which bone mass will be lost later in life. To prevent difficulties later in life, it's particularly important to build up bone density and to avoid bone loss in those first two decades of development.

What Happens If I Don't Take My Medication?

Remember . . . there can be consequences when you don't take drugs.

> **Take Action**
>
> If you or a loved one are dealing with epilepsy, ask your doctor whether the drugs being prescribed are known to increase bone loss. If so, see whether there's an alternative medication that can prevent that result. Since it takes a long time for osteoporosis to develop, we have complete information only about the older drugs and their side effects. In any case, it's a good idea for both children and adults to take calcium and vitamin D supplements, do antigravity exercises, and have periodic bone density scans. If bone loss is detected, you should ask about a referral to an endocrinologist or other specialist.

Most of us would rather not take drugs on a daily basis. But it's important to bear in mind that drugs aren't the only cause of side effects. An untreated medical condition, especially one as complex as epilepsy, can have serious side effects too. Injuries and problems dealing with the ordinary activities of daily life can easily occur if a person prone to seizures isn't properly medicated.

It's reassuring to know that antiseizure drugs pose virtually no long-term risks involving cancer, heart disease, and other serious conditions. Epileptologists consider the drugs listed in this chapter to be essentially nontoxic. They have long, successful track records, and people have taken them every day for many years without adverse outcomes.

What Is the Best Form of the Drug to Take?

Some adults and quite a number of children have trouble swallowing pills. It may be advisable to see whether the drug selected is provided in another form. Some medications are available in sprinkles that can be mixed into foods (such as applesauce), *dispersible tablets* that dissolve in the mouth, and liquids.

Some drugs have long-acting forms that may reduce the number of times each day that a person has to take them. Some drugs can even be administered just once a day.

Are the Medications Affordable?

Without a fairly comprehensive medical insurance plan, one that includes reimbursement for drugs, an individual might have difficulty affording antiepileptic prescription drugs. Costs can vary, however. Newer drugs are usually still under patent and will be more expensive, while the older drugs, which are often just as effective as newer drugs, are frequently available in generic form.

Talk with your doctor about the affordability issue, and explore solutions that don't require you to eliminate critically important medications. Some pharmaceutical companies have "compassionate use" programs that make drugs available to people who can't afford to pay, but these programs are difficult to find, and qualifying for them can be a daunting task.

What Is the Right Dose?

Once the right drug has been selected, it's crucial for the physician to determine the correct dose for the person taking it. If an individual is taking too low a dose, she may have a *breakthrough seizure* (unexpected seizure), and if the dose is too high she may experience side effects that would not occur at a lower dose level.

> ## Take Action
>
> Everyone—the person who has epilepsy and his relatives and friends—can help the medication process by following these simple steps:
>
> 1. Make sure the drug is taken exactly as prescribed. Use a weekly pill organizer to make sure that all the pills for every day are taken. Family members can help too, since everyone forgets sometimes.
>
> 2. Aim to take the medication at roughly the same time every day so that it becomes a habit. If you skip a dose accidentally, you can make it up later. But if you miss more than two doses, call your physician and ask how he would recommend proceeding.
>
> 3. If you've been taking the medication correctly and the seizures continue, or if you find that you're experiencing distressing side effects, contact your doctor immediately and see whether the dose should be adjusted or a different drug should be considered.

Every physician will begin drug therapy at a low or medium dosage level, in order to discover the smallest effective amount and avoid overshooting the optimum dose. Don't be discouraged if the seizures aren't immediately eliminated when a new drug is started. The dose may simply have to be raised slightly until the drug reaches the desired effect for that particular person's system.

Sometimes it takes time for the medication to build up in the body, and different drugs build up at different rates, based on the individual's metabolism. If the drug is producing unpleasant side effects, it may be wise to slow down the schedule for advancing the dosage and to allow the body to acclimate to the new medication.

Available Epilepsy Drugs

The alphabetical list below includes both the generic category of the drug and some of the available brand names in each category.

- **Adrenocorticotropin** (ah-DREE-no-core-tih-co-tro-pin): adrenocorticotropic hormone (ACTH), Acthar Gel (for infantile spasms)

- **Benzodiazepines** (ben-zo-die-AYZ-ah-peens): Clobazam (Onfi), Clonazepam (Klonopin), Clorazepate (Tranxene), Diazepam (Diastat, Valium), Lorazepam (Ativan), Midazolam (Versed)

- **Carbamazepine** (car-bah-MAZ-uh-peen): Carbatrol, Tegretol; **Oxcarbazepine** (ox-car-BAZ-up-peen): Trileptal; and **Eslicarbazepine** (ess-lee-car-BAZ-up-peen): Aptiom

- **Ethosuximide** (ee-tho-SUX-ih-mide): Zarontin

- **Ezogabine** (ee-ZOG-uh-been) (also called Retigabine in countries outside the U.S.): Potiga

- **Felbamate** (FELL-buh-mate): Felbatol

- **Gabapentin** (gab-uh-PEN-tin): Neurontin; and **Pregabalin** (pree-GAB-uh-lin): Lyrica

Take Action

After starting or changing a medication, be sure to ask your doctor how long it will be before you can expect your seizures to come under control.

> Also, it's a good idea to ask about the short- and medium-term side effects that you might experience, and bring up any special aspects of your lifestyle that could be negatively affected by those side effects. Remember, if you don't tell your physician, she won't know to adjust your medications.

- **Lacosamide** (la-KOSE-uh-mide): Vimpat

- **Lamotrigine** (la-MO-tra-gene): Lamictal

- **Levetiracetam** (lev-ih-tir-ASS-ih-tam): Keppra

- **Perampanel** (per-AMP-an-el): Fycompa

- **Phenobarbital** (fee-no-BAR-bit-all)

- **Phenytoin** (FEN-ih-toe-in): Dilantin; and **Fosphenytoin** (fos-FEN-ih-toe-in): Cerebyx

- **Primidone** (PRIM-ih-doan): Mysoline

- **Rufinamide** (ruh-FIN-uh-mide): Banzel

- **Tiagabine** (tye-AG-a-been): Gabitril

- **Topiramate** (toe-PIE-rah-mate): Topamax, Trokendi, Qudexy

- **Valproate** (VAL-pro-ate): Depakote, Depakene

- **Vigabatrin** (vi-GAB-ah-trin): Sabril

- **Zonisamide** (zoe-NISS-ah-mide): Zonegran

Take Action

Talk to your doctor about any medications you may be taking so that he can consider possible drug interactions. He may have to consult with other physicians, such as a cancer specialist and a neurologist. Your doctor may decide to check the level in your blood of all the drugs you're taking to be sure that everything is being kept in balance.

Drug Interactions

There are times when antiepileptic drugs can react negatively with other drugs you may be taking, or vice versa. Or both situations can happen simultaneously. So your doctor must know about these complicated possibilities before she prescribes anything for you.

For example, some antiepileptic drugs can speed up the body's normal breakdown of birth control pills, so a person might have to take a higher dose of estrogen or use other forms of contraception to compensate. On the other hand, hormonal birth control pills can speed up the breakdown of an antiepileptic medication so that an increase in the seizure medicine may be needed. Finding the right balance is crucial.

Some of the drugs that can cause these interactions include:

- Birth control pills
- Blood thinners or anticlotting drugs
- Drugs used after transplant surgery
- Medications used for other serious illnesses

When Does Medication End?

When we make a decision to start medication, it's usually not a lifelong decision. All drug therapy should be reevaluated as time goes by, and if you have no seizures for several years, it might be a good idea to consider stopping the drugs. However, if the underlying cause of the epilepsy isn't likely to disappear, your physician may recommend continuing the medications, even if seizures have ceased.

If you've had no seizures for several years and a new EEG shows no worrisome findings, you and your family should discuss with your physician the possibility of concluding drug therapy. Choices can depend on circumstances. Some people, such as parents of young children and young women planning a family, may be more motivated than others to stop the medications. Others may prefer to continue the drugs, appreciating the reassurance of being able to continue their lifestyles uninterrupted.

What You Should Know

- The most important question is the most obvious: will the drug work for your type of epilepsy? The choice narrows further when possible side effects are considered in connection with your specific case.

- While taking drugs does have side effects, consequences can also occur when you *don't* take drugs that might help.

- Carefully monitor drug dosage and make sure that you take medication exactly as prescribed.

Chapter 5

When Medications Aren't Working

When medications are taken as prescribed and they're not working, four main possibilities are considered:

1. The drug dose is too low. Since virtually every physician aims to use enough medicine but not more than enough, doses are usually low at the start. The good news is that some people will stop having epileptic seizures at relatively low doses of medication.

2. The wrong drug has been prescribed to treat a particular kind of epilepsy. Sometimes the initial diagnosis is based in large degree on historical information, which may be slightly inaccurate. This can occasionally result in medications that have little or no positive effect. With more

testing, a physician can sometimes identify a specific kind of epilepsy and pinpoint the proper drug.

3. Some epilepsies can't really be "fixed" or helped adequately by drug therapy. Surprising as it may seem in the 21st century, there are still some epilepsies that do not respond well to any of the medications on the market. Current estimates indicate that 60 percent of epilepsies can be treated effectively through moderate doses of medication. But that means that approximately 40 percent of patients will have epilepsy that is *refractory*, or difficult to control with drugs, usually from the outset. Fortunately, some of these individuals can obtain relief from surgery or other interventions, such as the *ketogenic diet* or *vagus nerve stimulation* (see pages 71–72 for more information).

4. The problem really isn't epilepsy at all, but some other type of medical or psychological condition that requires an entirely different kind of treatment program.

In Denise's case, the first drug chosen to treat the seizures was not the most effective. Obtaining more information led to a positive change.

Denise
Paul and Pamela never really understood how their ten-year-old daughter, Denise, became such a baseball fanatic. But the fact was that she loved her hometown team, the Cleveland Indians, and was a star shortstop on her team, Greased Lightning.

As good as she was at snagging line drives and picking up hot grounders, there were times when Denise just seemed to zone out. Now and then she would stare off into space and smack her lips. These episodes lasted a few seconds or so. Immediately afterward she would be slightly confused, and a few seconds after that she'd be fine. Pamela noticed that these events occurred several times a week.

A neurologist gave Denise an EEG test, which came back normal, as did the subsequent MRI scan. On the basis of the girl's history, the doctor sensibly prescribed a particular drug. But the staring episodes not only continued, they worsened progressively and became more frequent. One day, Denise's staring actually evolved into a grand mal convulsion.

Denise's parents then decided to seek a second opinion, and that's when I saw their daughter for the first time. I spoke to her first doctor on the phone, and he indicated that on the basis of her parents' description of the episodes, he had initially believed that Denise might be experiencing focal epileptic seizures. I recommended a longer EEG, which lasted about two hours after sleep deprivation. Denise was allowed fewer hours of sleep than usual the night before the test, and when she came in for her EEG, she was ready for a nap. This was helpful because sometimes the EEG abnormalities are best seen when the person is sleeping. This time, the EEG showed evidence of generalized epilepsy.

With this additional information, I was able to prescribe a drug targeted at resolving generalized epileptic seizures, and Denise soon was able to resume her passion for baseball without the interruptions of staring episodes, or worse.

What Factors Determine a Dosage Adjustment?

Some people have medical conditions that prevent them from taking a high enough dose of a particular medication to provide relief from seizures. For instance, if a person has an allergic reaction to a drug, the medication must be discontinued. Of course, virtually everyone taking any drug at elevated dosage levels will experience one or more side effects. That's why doctors prescribing antiepileptic drugs must attempt to establish the lowest, most effective dose for each person.

Blood level tests can determine whether the patient is actually taking the prescribed medication. Some patients don't take their medications as scheduled (or even at all), and it's critical for the doctor to know this before mistakenly prescribing a higher dose that could result in adverse side effects. The blood level test can also indicate whether there's something unusual about the patient's metabolism that could be affecting how the drug is entering his system.

However, blood levels aren't the only measurement of how much medication should be prescribed. Most doctors use the patient's clinical response. That is, the physician monitors the impact the drug is having on seizures and what side effects occur, and makes adjustments accordingly. If seizures continue, the dosage will be increased until either the seizures stop or negative side effects begin to appear.

When it comes to drugs, the key concept involved is the therapeutic index, which refers to a dosage that's high enough to work but not so high that it creates toxic side effects. The therapeutic index for every person and every drug is different, and that's why dosages are absolutely individual.

Take Action

> If seizures continue despite treatment, don't just "settle" and decide to accept the situation. First, be sure that you're seeing a board-certified specialist in epilepsy, since board-certified specialists will know about all the available treatment options. If everything is "okay," but you still experience ongoing seizures or drug side effects, be sure to explore all your options. There may be a higher level of well-being you can experience with the right treatment.
>
> And remember, if you're reading about epilepsy on the Internet, you may be encountering a lot of unreliable information.

How Are Drugs Switched When One Drug Isn't Working?

In a case such as Denise's (page 66), when one drug is being replaced with another, the doctor will often recommend an overlap of the two drugs. The first drug will be phased out over a period of time as the new drug is slowly introduced. This provides the patient with some protection as the second drug builds up its presence in the body. If the second drug shows promise, the first drug is taken away completely.

At times during these transitions, if doses are too low, there can be breakthrough seizures. Or there may be side effects from an interaction between the two drugs. So dosage levels may need to be fine-tuned to minimize these effects. As a result, transition from one drug to another can take time, sometimes a matter of weeks.

Take Action

Don't be alarmed if your doctor's first step in response to your continuing seizures is to increase the dosage. Remember that the doctor probably started on the low side and has room to go up before any side effects are experienced. Still, it's important to ask your doctor what kind of side effects she'll be looking for as the drug dosage is increased. This will help you monitor the drug therapy process as well and will assist your physician to find the proper medication balance quickly. If the maximum clinically tolerable dosage is ineffective, then the next step may be to switch medications.

Should More Than One Drug Be Used?

Usually, a doctor won't commit to multiple drug therapy right away, since there are some benefits to following a simpler one-drug program of treatment if that is possible. However, there are some two-drug combinations that can be more effective than either drug used alone. The doctor just has to monitor the side effects closely to make sure the drugs aren't interacting in a negative way.

However, as a general rule, it's unwise to use several medications at one time or to use one drug after another on a continuing basis. Side effects can accumulate faster than the positive effects on seizure control. Usually, if the seizure control is the same, people feel better on simpler one- or two-drug regimens. That is, if a person is taking one drug and has three seizures a month, and then starts taking two or three drugs but still has three seizures a month, he would be better off with the one-drug regimen.

What If Dosages Have Been Adjusted and/or Drugs Have Been Switched and There Is Still No Improvement?

Even if the patient still experiences seizures, it's possible that the drug(s) may be having a partial positive effect. We see this effect when we bring a patient to the hospital and take her off medication to induce a seizure for purposes of studying the dynamics of the epilepsy. There are times when the patient's family is surprised at the increased intensity or frequency of the seizures in the absence of medication.

Of course, it can be discouraging when there aren't enough positive results and the person is troubled by side effects. At this point, it's time for another approach.

Take Action

If you're not seeing positive results and you're experiencing numerous side effects, at this point, you should request a referral to a comprehensive epilepsy center. The doctors at such a center will review the case from the beginning and will probably recommend a video EEG, MRI, and other testing to obtain the most accurate clinical information about the seizures. Once the facts have been analyzed, the physicians may have new ideas about medication, or they may recommend surgery or alternative treatment options.

Alternative Treatments

The ketogenic diet and vagus nerve stimulation are two alternative treatments that may be considered for treating epilepsy. While these therapies may offer advantages to an individual, it's relatively uncommon for such treatments to result in the complete elimination of seizures. Furthermore, each of these therapies carries its own risks, which explains why most physicians explore treatment with drugs or with surgery, if that's an option, before pursuing alternative therapies.

Ketogenic Diet

The ketogenic diet actually changes the body's chemistry, which can be measured by blood and urine tests. For some people, the change can have a calming effect on seizures and can reduce or even eliminate the need for antiepileptic drugs. This stringent diet is high in fat and low in carbohydrates and protein, forcing the body to burn fat instead of glucose for energy and creating a new chemical state.

Maintaining this new chemical state requires an absolutely rigid adherence to the diet particulars since even a minor dietary indiscretion will reverse the new body chemistry. This is one reason that the ketogenic diet is often used for younger children whose diets are more easily controlled, rather than for teenagers or adults. Modified, less stringent high-fat diets are also being explored, but their effects haven't been established.

Families attempting this treatment option must be highly motivated and committed to changing their lifestyle and eating style, possibly for a long time (usually up to two years). The diet should be coordinated with a specialized dietitian connected with an epilepsy center, someone who understands all the ramifications of such a treatment program and can help the family implement the treatment.

There are some genetic and metabolic conditions that would preclude the use of the ketogenic diet. Testing before the diet is begun will reveal whether it can be used. Possible complications include reduced bone mass, kidney stones, and impaired growth.

Vagus Nerve Stimulation (VNS)

Vagus nerve stimulation can assist in interrupting or avoiding a potential seizure. It calls for the implantation under general anesthesia of a small generator in the upper left area of the chest. The generator can be programmed to provide electrical stimulation to the vagus nerve in the neck through a connecting wire. That signal then travels into the brain on a short cyclical schedule and with an intensity determined by the doctor. Patients who experience a warning before a seizure occurs can initiate the generator's action themselves by waving a magnet over the area where the generator is implanted, or with some devices the stimulation may be triggered automatically when a sensory registers a sudden increase in the heart rate. Often, this extra stimulation enables the device to stop the seizure in progress.

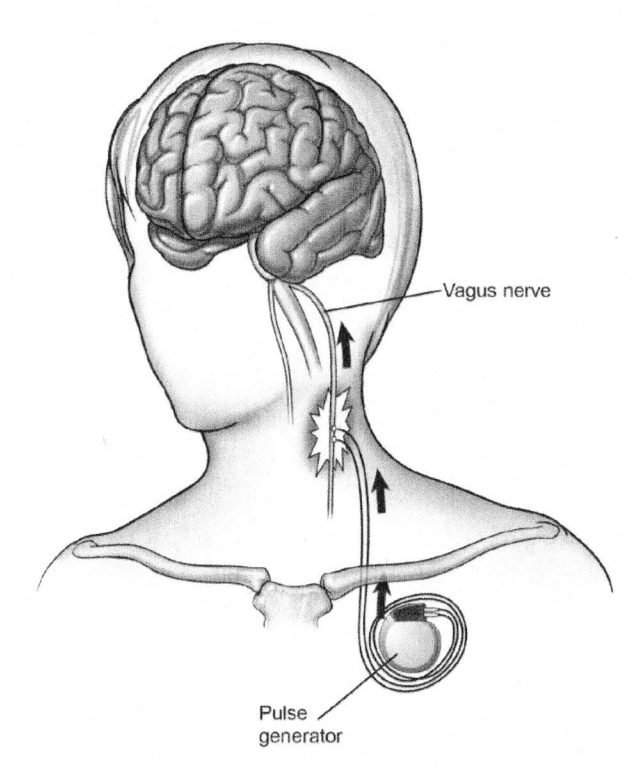

Figure 5.1. *The vagus nerve stimulator intermittently passes a light electrical current up into the brain via one of the vagus nerves in the neck. For some people with epilepsy, this helps to reduce the seizures.*

There are some risks connected with VNS. These include infection, minor follow-up surgeries for battery replacement, and the potential impact on MRI scans (since the metal in the VNS wire and generator could affect such scans). Also, coughing, hoarseness, and swallowing difficulties have been reported by people when the device is stimulating the nerve.

On the positive side, some people like the empowerment of being able to intercede as a seizure is beginning and, potentially, being able to stop the seizure by activating the generator.

If vagus nerve stimulation doesn't work, the generator can be removed, but the wire is usually left in place to avoid any nerve damage that might occur during its removal.

Are Clinical Trials a Good Option?

Participants in a clinical trial may not know whether they're receiving the actual drug or temporarily receiving a sugar pill (placebo). In such trials, either the placebo or the new drug is added to an established antiepileptic medication. The placebo is used to show the outcomes of a control group of participants not receiving the medication compared to the outcomes of similar patients receiving the drug. Safety will always be a high priority in every study design. Any potential risks posed by the experimental drug will be discussed thoroughly in the informed consent process and documented in writing.

Take Action

Inquire about any clinical trials that the person with epilepsy might qualify for, including trials involving new medications and innovative devices. Most specialized epilepsy centers have information regarding these clinical trials and can provide information about participation.

Be sure the trial is conducted by qualified physicians at a respected medical center and that the study has been analyzed for ethical

> compliance and safety by an institutional review board. Ask your physician if you have any questions.

Note: If a person receives the placebo instead of the drug during the clinical trial, the active drug will be made available to that individual at the conclusion of the trial if it's found that the drug is safe and tolerable. Of course, if a participant's seizures worsen at any point during the study, that person will be removed from the trial and he'll be examined to make sure there are no adverse consequences.

If a person is accepted into a clinical trial, there's usually no cost for either the treatment or any additional testing. Participants often feel that they're helping to advance the study and treatment of epilepsy.

What about Out-of-the-Mainstream Therapies?

There are a number of out-of-the-mainstream therapeutic approaches for people with epilepsy, some of which you may discover on the Internet. These might include herbal treatments, aromatherapy, and some brand-name concoctions. Discuss with your doctor any particular treatment that interests you before you try it, since the new therapy could cause complications with existing drugs or could put you at risk in other ways.

Your physician can help provide any scientific data that might exist about this nonstandard therapy. It is well to remember, however, that in many cases these treatments haven't been studied at all in a scientifically controlled environment. As a result, the promised benefits are only unverified statements and not proven outcomes.

One of the most frequently used or considered out-of-the-mainstream treatments for epilepsy is medical marijuana, or CBD (cannabidiol). Although the drug has not been fully researched or approved by the US Food and Drug Administration, impressive results have been reported by some families, with improved seizure control. For persons experiencing uncontrolled epilepsy who wish to explore CBD, the safest way for now is to apply for participation in an approved research study under the supervision of a certified epilepsy specialist.

Of course, there are some treatment options that are harmless as far as anyone can tell. The key here is to make sure you won't be doing more damage. Your physician will be able to help you make that determination.

What Everyone Should Know

- There are four reasons drugs may not be working, so make sure you explore all the possibilities before jumping to conclusions.

- As a general rule, using more than two drugs at the same time is not as beneficial as using one or two that have been shown to be effective.

- If drugs aren't working, consult with your doctor about the possibility of trying other treatments, such as epilepsy surgery (see next chapter), the ketogenic diet, and vagus nerve stimulation.

- Some untested therapies can do more harm than good.

Chapter 6

Epilepsy Surgery

In the past, some doctors believe that surgery should be used only as a last resort for people with epilepsy, after almost all the available medications and alternative therapies have been attempted. Other physicians see surgery as a very positive option for the subgroup of people who are good candidates, even if only some of the available medications have been tried.

Successful surgery can often eliminate many of the lifestyle constraints epilepsy imposes, including the inability to drive, repeated hospital visits, the reduction of professional opportunities, added family stress, and limitations to other daily activities. If the first few medications—used appropriately and at adequate doses—have failed to control the seizures, subsequent medical trials are unlikely to solve the problem.

Nowadays, the average period a patient lives with uncontrolled seizures before surgery is attempted is approximately ten years. Many of us see this as an unnecessarily long time for a patient to suffer the consequences of seizures if surgery is a viable option for that person. For example, Tony had seizures for 14 years before he was referred for surgery at our Epilepsy Center.

Tony

As head coach of a successful mid-level college football team, the Wooster University Wildcats, Tony was immersed in his sport all year long. When he wasn't on the sidelines during a game or supervising drills on the practice field, he was busy visiting high schools to grade and recruit prospects for the future. As a result, the 41-year-old father of three didn't see his family as much as he would have liked.

But that wasn't the only challenge Tony faced. When he was 27 he had begun having epileptic seizures. They were complex partial seizures with automatisms, which meant that he could feel a "rising" sensation in his stomach just before blacking out. Witnesses reported that during a seizure, Tony would stare, smack his lips, and make fumbling movements with his fingers. The seizures usually lasted for a few minutes, and afterward Tony was temporarily confused and sleepy, with no memory of what had happened during the episode. A few of his seizures had progressed into grand mal events.

An EEG test showed sharp waves, indicating that Tony might have right temporal lobe epilepsy. The first MRI scan appeared normal, so he was put on a drug-therapy program that seemed to reduce the frequency and intensity of the seizures, eliminating the grand mal seizures.

But as time passed, the seizures began occurring more often, and by the time I saw him, Tony was experiencing three or four episodes a month. This meant that he couldn't drive, which posed a particular difficulty for him. What with all the recruiting trips and late nights at the field house, public transportation wasn't a good option for Tony. He needed to be able to come and go anywhere at any hour. And occasionally he had to manage the embarrassment of having a seizure in front of his team or coaching staff. Tony's wife, Katherine, was understanding and supportive, but his epilepsy clearly added stress to their lives.

Tony and I discussed his history, including the four drugs he had taken for substantial periods of time. They had had some good effects, but had not come close enough to eliminating his seizures. I scheduled a new MRI for Tony, and it revealed that his right hippocampus was shrunken and sclerotic (or hardened), which meant that it didn't look healthy.

Hippocampal sclerosis (see page 46) can be rather subtle in appearance and may not be found in standard MRI scans that aren't programmed to examine closely for hippocampus abnormalities. As is often the case, we didn't know why Tony had hippocampal sclerosis, but we did know that surgery could often help. To better understand his treatment options, we brought Tony into the hospital, temporarily took him off medication, and conducted a video EEG. We then recorded a seizure that clearly originated in his right temporal lobe.

Neuropsychological testing raised no additional concerns, so Tony and I discussed the pros and cons of epilepsy surgery. I told Tony that the test results indicated that he was an excellent candidate for removal of the hippocampus and some of the surrounding material in the temporal lobe.

I estimated that there was a 75 percent chance that we could remove the trigger zone for his epilepsy and achieve complete freedom from seizures. We would continue his medications for up to two years after surgery, and if he had no seizures in that time, medications could probably be withdrawn. At the least, I told him that the surgery could make his epilepsy more controllable.

Of course, I also informed Tony about the risks of brain surgery, including a less than 2 percent chance of an anesthesia complication, bleeding, infection, stroke, or other serious problems. Those risks are statistically quite low, and our medical center had a particularly good track record for brain surgery free of those complications. And in Tony's case, the surgery would take place in an area of the brain that was already damaged; the surgery would not leave him with any new deficits in terms of motor functioning, language, memory, or other abilities.

Tony decided to go forward with the surgery, and he was out of the hospital in four days. There were no complications, and his mild and temporary postsurgical headaches were treated with over-the-counter pain medication. He was back on the practice field in a month, just in time for spring workouts with his Wildcats. Five years later, he still hasn't had a single seizure, even though antiepileptic medications had been stopped two years after surgery.

Who Is a Good Candidate for Surgery?

In determining who is an appropriate candidate for surgery, the doctor will first try to determine whether there's a focal trigger zone for the seizures. In theory, if that one zone of the brain is removed, the seizures will stop. If a patient's seizure symptoms, EEG, and MRI tests do not indicate focal epilepsy, that person isn't likely to benefit from surgery.

Common causes of epilepsies that can often be treated with surgery include:

- Hippocampal sclerosis
- Tumor
- Focal brain malformation
- Previous stroke in a focal area
- Previous focal injury from trauma or infection
- Other specialized conditions

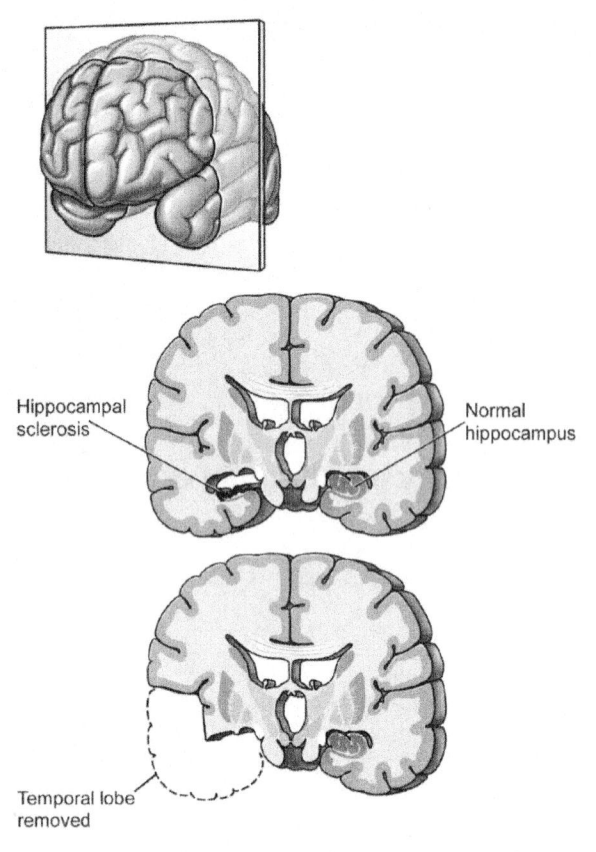

Figure 6.1. *Hippocampal sclerosis is seen on the MRI as shrinkage and scarring of the hippocampus on the inside of the temporal lobe. When this presents on one side only, removing the hippocampus and surrounding temporal lobe may provide relief from seizures.*

The second criterion for surgery calls for a determination of whether that focal zone is located in an area of the brain that can be removed safely, without causing loss of function. For example, if the person has normal motor function and his seizures are beginning right in the middle of the motor region, removing the trigger zone may result in a degradation of motor functioning.

The relative benefits and risks of any surgery vary from one case to the next, and all the factors must be weighed by the physician and patient. These factors could include the severity of the epilepsy as well as the lifestyle of the patient. For instance, a few seizures a month may be a more serious disability for one person than for another, depending on each individual's specific circumstances. Similarly, an expected side effect of a particular surgery (for example, a loss of peripheral vision) may pose significant difficulties for some while it isn't a major issue for others. These concerns must be addressed carefully in every case.

Quality of life is the bottom line when it comes to making a decision about surgery. The seizures themselves need not be frequent or violent for surgery to be considered.

In Tony's case, most of his seizures were not grand mal convulsions. But the unpredictable nature of the episodes and the fact that they included loss of awareness had an enormous impact on his life and career path. So surgery became the preferable choice.

There's no "right" age for epilepsy surgery. Infants and senior citizens, as well as everyone in between, could be excellent surgical candidates, depending on their individual circumstances.

Take Action

If your seizures aren't controlled or impose difficult challenges in your career or personal life, ask your doctor whether surgery is an option. If you're not sure that you're getting a clear answer, request a referral for a second opinion.

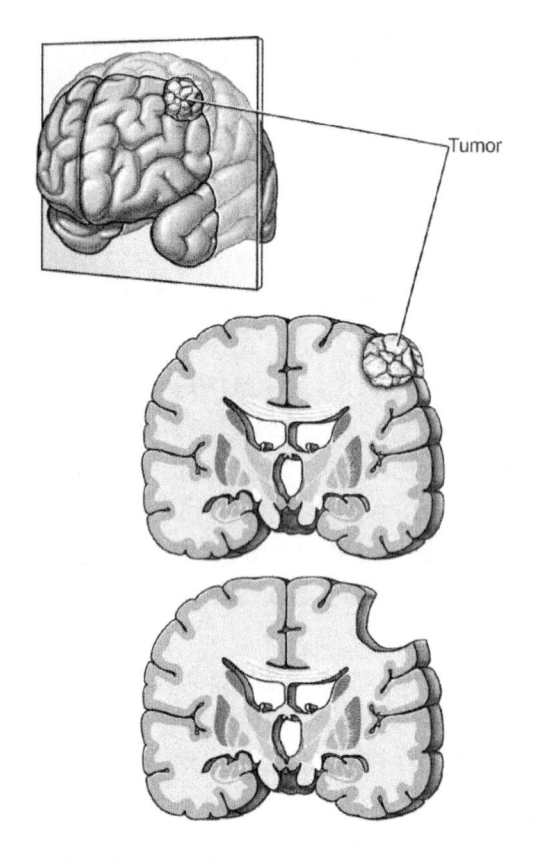

Figure 6.2. *When an MRI reveals the cause of the epilepsy to be a tumor, the next step is often to remove it with surgery.*

The idea is to shorten the time between believing that surgery is a good idea and actually getting it done. If the first few drugs don't work, it's highly unlikely that the next several medications will be any more effective.

Considering Surgery Is Not a Commitment to Having the Surgery

As already stated, if a person with epilepsy has tried a few drugs and given them a fair chance to work out over time, and if they still aren't working, she may want to explore the surgical option. However, this in no way commits her to following through with the surgery. She should simply inform her doctor that she wants to find out whether she's a viable candidate. While this may involve traveling to an epilepsy center for a second opinion, it's not an irrevocable step. The patient will have plenty of time to weigh the pros and cons of surgery before coming to a decision.

Take Action

Sometimes, even without hospital testing, it's possible for a person experiencing seizures or his family to see clear indications that he exhibits the first criterion for surgery, focal epilepsy. As discussed in chapter 1, focal epilepsies are often accompanied by an aura, or motor or sensory involvement of one part of the body or either side of the body. A person also may know that he experienced brain trauma or stroke at some point in his life that resulted in a localized injury, or an MRI may have shown a focal malformation or tumor.

If any of these indications is present, you should speak to your doctor about surgical alternatives. This, in turn, may lead to your finding a second opinion.

Even when these clues aren't present, epilepsy surgery may still help. If medications aren't solving the problem, it's always a good idea to ask your neurologist whether a presurgical evaluation should be considered.

Second Opinions for Epilepsy Surgery

The starting point for this process is a comprehensive epilepsy center equipped with a video EEG unit. New noninvasive tests will be performed, including another MRI scan and a video EEG, each conducted with special protocols targeting the suspected focal trigger zone of the brain.

The video EEG is a specially equipped unit designed to observe and monitor an epilepsy patient 24 hours a day for several days. With a video recording running continuously, physicians can observe any seizures that occur and at the same time analyze the brain waves both during seizures and at other times while the person is asleep and awake.

Unless the seizures are happening on a daily basis, the center may facilitate the recording of a seizure by reducing or stopping any medication. (The video EEG unit is a safe environment where the patient is monitored constantly and can be attended to immediately when a seizure occurs.)

If the video EEG and MRI match and indicate a particular trigger zone, there may be no need for further testing. If questions remain, further testing may include:

- **PET (positron emission tomography) scans**. *PET scans* can detect abnormal patterns of brain function using a weakly radioactive substance that is administered by intravenous injection during a nonseizure time.

- **Ictal SPECT (single photon emission computed tomography) scans**. *Ictal SPECT scans* are similar to PET scans. The difference is that another radioactive substance is injected during a seizure.

- **Magnetoencephalography**. *Magnetoencephalography* can help localize the origin of abnormal EEG discharges (sharp waves) by pinpointing magnetic fields generated by the brain.

After the testing is completed, if the patient is being considered for surgery, often a board or committee (including the epilepsy specialists, epilepsy neurosurgeons, radiologists, nurses, and psychologists) will meet to review the results.

If the board members agree that surgery is appropriate, it's possible that a full surgical plan can be developed as a result of the noninvasive testing that has just been completed. In some cases, however, invasive testing will be recommended.

Invasive Testing

Most people don't need invasive testing, since the noninvasive tests will usually reveal everything the surgeon needs to know.

Sometimes, however, special questions must still be answered, questions that will require another level of testing, including invasive testing. This may involve mapping the area of the brain for surgery and clearly identifying the areas of language and motor function in relation to the area of the brain that is triggering seizure activity.

Such mapping is most often performed in two surgical stages. During the first surgery, while the patient is under anesthesia, a section of the skull is opened and a plastic sheet that is implanted with electrodes is left directly on the brain. The section of bone is then replaced over the sheet, and the electrode wires are brought outside the skull for connection to the monitoring equipment. Over the next three to five days, while the individual is awake and alert, the implanted electrodes will be used to record subsequent seizures.

These electrodes can also be used to map areas of the brain that control various body functions, such as speech and language. A mild electric current is passed through the electrodes into different brain regions to see whether the patient can interact and move certain parts of his body during stimulation. The procedure isn't painful or uncomfortable, but the entire process requires a high level of cooperation between patient and physician.

Once the mapping is complete, the individual returns to surgery and is anesthetized. The bone section is removed, the plastic sheet with electrodes is taken off the brain, and the brain surgery proceeds on the basis of the information gained from the mapping. If everything goes well, the patient usually leaves the hospital within five to seven days.

Alternatively, in some situations the doctor may decide to use stereotactic depth electrodes, which are introduced into the brain under MRI guidance through small holes in the skull. This is done while the patient is under anesthesia. By recording brain activity, the electrodes help determine where the seizures originate.

Occasionally, the mapping and surgery can take place at the same time, in one step, but this requires the patient to be awake during part of the procedure. The procedures performed while the patient is awake do not hurt since there are no pain sensors in the brain.

Types of Epilepsy Surgery

There are several types of epilepsy surgery.

Lesionectomy or Focal Resection

With a *lesionectomy*, a small part of the brain is removed or *resected*, as in the removal of Tony's hippocampus or the removal of a tumor. The piece of brain could be as small as a child's marble, but is often larger. In other cases, an entire region of the brain might be removed, such as much of one lobe (called a lobectomy) or even multiple lobes next to each other on one side.

Hemispherectomy

In a *hemispherectomy*, an entire hemisphere of the brain is removed or disconnected from the rest of the brain. In hemispherectomy candidates, who are usually children, the epilepsy tends to be severe and the damaged side of the brain is doing far more harm than good.

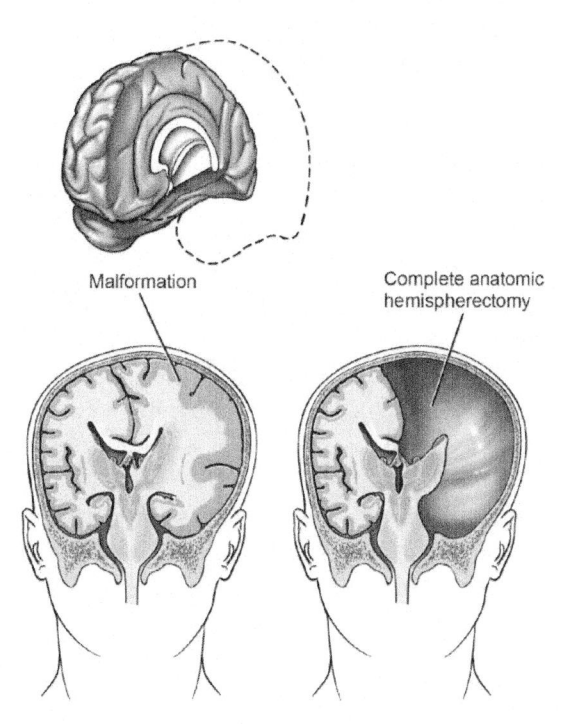

Figure 6.3. *A complete hemispherectomy may be the best approach to dealing with uncontrollable epilepsy caused by a large malformation of part or all of one side of the brain. In this procedure, the neurosurgeon removes almost all of the affected half of the brain.*

While a hemispherectomy sounds drastic, some of our best and most gratifying results are achieved in these types of surgeries, with a 70 to 80 percent chance for eliminating seizures. Candidates for this procedure already have hemiparesis (weakness on one side of the body) due to the underlying brain malformation or injury. Since this typically happened very early in life, the person's language skills developed on the other side—so removing or disconnecting the damaged or malformed hemisphere does not result in new language or motor problems.

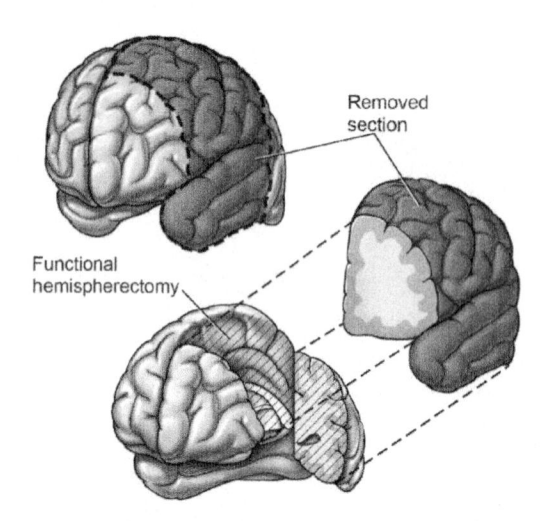

Figure 6.4. *Functional hemispherectomy may be ideal for uncontrolled epilepsy resulting from stroke or other lesions limited to one side of the brain. The neurosurgeon removes a large section of the abnormal hemisphere and disconnects the remaining areas on that side from the rest of the brain.*

Other Specialized Surgeries

Other quite rare surgical procedures are performed only in very special situations. These include:

- **Corpus callosotomy**. The *corpus callosotomy* divides the connection between the two brain hemispheres to reduce, but usually not stop, seizure frequency.

- **Removal of hypothalamic hamartoma**. This involves removal of a benign growth, called a *hypothalamic* *hamartoma*, deep inside the brain, near structures involved with vision and hormone function. In some cases the hamartoma may be inactivated by gamma-knife radiosurgery or laser surgery. **Laser surgery** may also be used to inactivate certain other types of localized brain abnormalities.

- **Responsive neurostimulation**. In special cases, long-term implanted electrodes may deliver electrical stimulation at seizure onset to a "trigger zone" that cannot be removed.

Complications from Surgery

Everyone should understand in advance that there are some risks and complications that occur with surgery. For example, in the attempt to remove the troublesome area, it also might be necessary for the surgeon to remove a part of the brain involved in a body function, such as peripheral vision. Such an outcome would be discussed in detail beforehand. There are also general risks attendant upon any neurosurgery—infection, stroke, bleeding, anesthesia complications—but those risks should be low (generally below 2 to 5 percent of all surgeries performed).

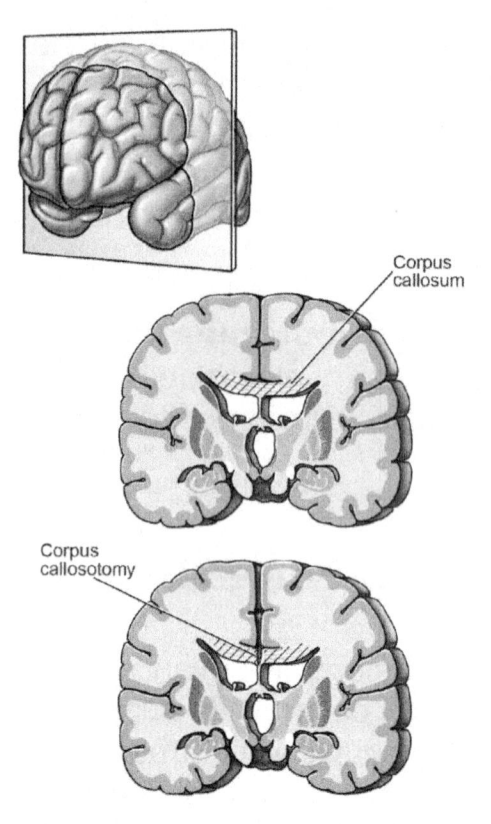

Figure 6.5. *Corpus callosotomy involves cutting the huge fiber bundle that connects the two hemispheres.*

Your best protection against such risks is to choose a center that has a respected team, a good track record, and a relatively high volume of patients like you.

Take Action

Since surgery involves a lot of interpretation of test results, think ahead when you choose an epilepsy center. If you think surgery may be a future option, you want to be at a center where epilepsy surgery is performed frequently and successfully.

In order to pick the best center, when you call or visit, ask whom you should talk to about your concerns. Then consider asking for the following information:

- The volume of surgeries compared to those done at other epilepsy centers

- Whether the center specializes in treating your particular type of epilepsy. (For example, my center specializes in surgery for pediatric as well as adult epilepsy.)

- Whether the center has all the technology and subspecialists required

- Whether the center is respected in the field and its physicians are board certified

- The number of epilepsy surgeries your surgeon performs in a year and what percentage of her practice is devoted to epilepsy surgery, as well as whether she's board certified

- The outcomes of specific surgeries—especially the percentage of patients with your type of epilepsy who experienced a total elimination of seizures after surgery

- The center's complication rate

Also, be sure you're completely comfortable with the informed consent process. Did you get all the information you need about the risks and benefits? Did you receive written material you could study? Were you able to ask all the questions you have and did you receive complete and satisfactory answers?

If you feel that you're receiving good advice from a respected center and doctor, you may not need a second opinion. But if you have any remaining questions or uncertainties, be sure to seek a second opinion from a top-quality source.

Take Action

See whether there's an epilepsy support group for parents or patients in your area, or explore the possibility of finding one on the Internet. While you should always take the information you find in these groups with a grain of salt, sharing your concerns with others can elicit an important source of support as well as a consumer's point of view regarding all aspects of epilepsy, including surgery. If there's no formal group, ask whether you can speak with other parents, caregivers, or patients who are dealing with epilepsy issues like yours.

Try to determine from your doctor whether you are in the mainstream of epilepsy patients or whether you'll require an unusual procedure. If it's the latter, you may need to do some research to find the center and the doctors who specialize in your specific condition. It's worth the work to find that center because it may make a big difference in your outcome. In short, get to the right place and then trust what they tell you. The appendix at the end of this book will give you a head start in your research.

What to Expect after Surgery

For most people, the seizures stop immediately after surgery. The first week or two may show some postsurgical seizure activity, but then it quiets down.

If you continue to be free of seizure, your medications may be scaled back. But usually your physician will recommend that you stay on some form of moderate drug therapy for a year or two to ensure that you're protected. Progress is often reassessed at six-month intervals. If there are no seizures and everything looks good, drugs may eventually be discontinued. Of course, if seizures reappear, you'll be put back on medications.

Sometimes seizures can recur as late as eight to ten years after surgery. Often, they can be stopped by medicine alone. And in the vast majority of cases, good outcomes remain good—permanently.

Why Surgery Might Not Work

As they say, "Nothing is 100 percent." For some people, surgery does not completely resolve the epileptic seizures. Sometimes that's because the entire trigger zone couldn't be removed since it overlapped crucial functional areas of the brain involving motor skills or language. Perhaps the surgeon did not realize how big the trigger zone was. Or perhaps too much brain tissue remained in place for other technical reasons, causing further seizures.

In these cases, a follow-up operation may be a possibility, and often such an approach is quite effective. Video EEG evaluation can help show more precisely whether further surgery is a good idea. If the seizures arise from an area that cannot be safely removed, your physician will structure an ongoing medical treatment plan using all other resources at his command.

What If Surgery Is Not an Option?

Sometimes we come to the end of the presurgical evaluation process and decide that the surgery would not be helpful—that is, the surgery itself would not effectively stop the seizures, the trigger zone cannot be removed safely, or the risks of surgery outweigh the risks posed by the particular epilepsy.

Then we proceed down a different path, with a focus on giving the patient the best quality of life possible. The physician will go back over all the treatments that have been tried and identify those that provided the best seizure control with the fewest side effects.

For example, a person may be taking three drugs and still having seizures along with some staggering side effects. It may be wiser to cut back to one or two drugs and improve quality of life by reducing the side effects. Or a patient may be taking a new drug but may actually have felt better on a previous medication. This may be the time to move back to the previous drug for the sake of making daily life easier.

Remember, though, that the medications may be helping more than you think, even if seizures still occur. If medications are stopped altogether, the seizures may become much more frequent or intense than usual.

Are Clinical Trials a Good Option?

If medications or alternative therapies are failing or if they don't seem right for you, and if epilepsy surgery isn't an option, there are sometimes experimental or innovative therapies available in clinical trials. These drugs or devices will already have been through animal trials, so there exists a body of information about their safety and effectiveness. And usually the drugs will have been used by some people, either in small test scenarios or in larger populations.

While these treatments are still in the process of receiving full scrutiny by government agencies, it appears likely that they will be approved. A person may gain access to such treatments by enrolling in a clinical study, which would require meeting certain specific criteria that the study demands.

What You Should Know

- Surgery is a positive option for those people with epilepsy who are good candidates for the procedure.

- If your neurologist has recommended an evaluation for surgery, check to see that you will be at a center with extensive experience and a good track record.

- There are different epilepsy surgeries for different kinds of epilepsy.

- As with medications, there are risks connected with both having surgery and not having surgery.

Part Three

Epilepsy in Children, Seniors, and Women

Chapter 7

Epilepsy in Children

While a child may have any of the seizure types that an adult has, there are some seizures that occur with greater frequency in infants, children, and teenagers under the age of 18. In addition, these age groups have particular concerns when it comes to dealing with epileptic seizures and the treatment of epilepsy. There are special concerns connected with drug therapy, different underlying causes, and the often unique ways that epilepsy appears in younger people.

Note: Some seizures (known as febrile seizures) that affect children aren't really epilepsy (see page 30). Brought on by fevers in infants and small children, these brief febrile seizures are most often characterized by loss of consciousness and the shaking or moving of the child's limbs on both sides of the body. Children who have febrile seizures are not considered to have epilepsy, since epilepsy is defined as two or more seizures that are not directly triggered by a fever or other provocation. Medication is usually not required to treat febrile seizures, which usually disappear by age five or six.

For some children with epilepsy, learning and development are especially important. My patient Jeremy illustrates this point.

Jeremy

Everyone who met Jeremy liked him instantly. His smile could warm up a room. The fourth-grader loved telling knock-knock jokes. His favorite: "Knock, knock." "Who's there?" "Althea." "Althea who?" "Althea later, alligator!" After he launched one of his punch lines, his laughter was irresistible. Jeremy's parents, Ron and Monica, were aware that along with a keen sense of humor, their beloved son had a slight learning disability. But they were proud of the progress he was making.

Back when Jeremy was born, there had been complications surrounding his birth, and he had spent some time in the intensive care unit until he was able to fly on his own. Even though he was a little slow in learning to talk, Jeremy seemed to be doing well in his mainstream classroom, where he received special attention for his learning issues. In light of his particular situation, his achievements were good enough to keep him moving along through the grades.

However, at age six, Jeremy experienced his first epileptic seizure. One day, his teacher noticed that Jeremy was looking to the right side and his right arm was jerking; when she called his name, he didn't answer. The jerking quickly increased in intensity and spread to his right leg and the right side of his face. At this point, Jeremy went into a grand mal convulsion, and although the entire event only lasted a few minutes, it was frightening for everyone who witnessed it.

By the time Jeremy arrived at the hospital emergency room, he was coming out of the seizure and was able to greet his parents, who had been summoned by the school. His only aftereffect was a headache that didn't seem too bad. Jeremy was transferred to my care at Cleveland Clinic.

The MRI I ordered showed some evidence of brain damage that might have occurred at birth, during the time that he was having difficulties. The EEG suggested that Jeremy's epilepsy was originating in the left frontal lobe, where the injury had been indicated by the MRI.

Before I started Jeremy on a medication, I discussed his condition with Ron and Monica. First, they made it clear that they didn't want to interfere with Jeremy's ability to learn, since that had been something of a struggle. With this concern in mind, I selected a drug that I felt would help control the focal epileptic seizures while avoiding the negative side effects the boy's parents had mentioned.

I also had to figure in Jeremy's body weight and consider how fast, at his age, his body could break down and use the drug. This led to the initial dosage I called for on the prescription. A few weeks later, Jeremy had another seizure, so I increased the dosage, and after that he had no more seizures.

At follow-up visits over the next three years I learned that Jeremy had remained almost completely free of seizures and was tolerating his medication well. However, he was finding that the fourth grade was harder than second or third, and he was now falling behind in class. In addition, his ability to maintain attention in class seemed to be slipping.

Understandably, Jeremy's parents wanted to know whether these classroom problems were being caused by the epilepsy, the drug, or both. I told them that I had chosen a drug that normally would not cause these effects and that, on the plus side, the seizures had subsided. I also told Ron and Monica that Jeremy's learning difficulties might be due to an underlying cause that shows up differently in different school years, depending on the challenges posed by the schoolwork. In the fourth grade, the academic demands were accelerating, and Jeremy's long-standing problems with reading seemed to be slowing him down.

I recommended that Jeremy receive more neuropsychological testing to determine his strengths and weaknesses. With this information, he and his parents could work with the school to help address his problems. Those tests led to a diagnosis of some learning and attention deficits, and an individual educational plan was developed for him.

Who Treats Childhood Epilepsy?

Pediatricians routinely refer parents to pediatric neurologists whenever possible. While there are some pediatric neurologists who specialize in epilepsy, virtually all pediatric neurologists have experience dealing with epilepsy. However, in some communities there may not be any physicians specializing in pediatric neurology. This is why neurologists who typically work with adult patients will sometimes provide consultation to pediatricians.

With the help of some special sessions in a smaller group, Jeremy started making progress in reading and math. As a matter of fact, he is now making even better progress in school than he was before his epilepsy began. We talked about the option of prescribing medication for attention deficit disorder, but it hasn't seemed necessary.

While it's possible that Jeremy will probably always have epilepsy, we hope that medication will be able to stop the seizures for the long term. In his case, the epilepsy and the learning problems were two separate issues, and we dealt with them accordingly.

Types of Childhood Epilepsies

An epilepsy syndrome is a collection of various signs and symptoms that tend to appear among groups of affected persons, often emerging in childhood. By placing a child in a particular syndrome grouping, his doctor can sometimes more readily identify the proper testing, treatments, and prognosis for that individual child.

The syndromes are determined by several factors:

- What kind of seizure it is

- What type of abnormality is seen on EEG

- The age of the child

- Data relating to the child's medical and social history, physical examination, family history, and laboratory testing

People categorize epilepsies in different ways, but one method is by terming them focal or generalized. (See chapter 2.)

Following are some of the more common epilepsy syndromes that may occur in children.

Benign Focal Epilepsy of Childhood (Benign Partial Epilepsy or Benign Rolandic Epilepsy)

This special type of focal epilepsy often begins between ages 2 and 12, arising particularly in the 8- to 10-year-old range. It's benign, which means that it does little harm. Except for the seizures, affected children are usually normal in every other way, and the seizures tend to be brief, often occurring only during sleep. They may be focal motor type, with twitching, pulling, numbness, or tingling in one part of the body (usually the face or mouth). There also may be a secondary generalized tonic-clonic, or grand mal, type of seizure.

Although a grand mal seizure may not sound benign, in benign focal epilepsy, grand mal seizures tend to be infrequent, they occur at home when the child is asleep in bed, and they usually last only a couple of minutes. Best of all, the young person with benign focal epilepsy can be expected to outgrow the seizures during her teenage years.

Because this epilepsy is benign in so many ways, treatment usually isn't necessary. When the child's EEG shows the special type of abnormality that accompanies this epilepsy type, the doctor can be quite confident about the diagnosis. What a relief for the worried parents!

In a typical case, a mother visits me with her clearly healthy and bright eight-year-old son. He's a bit irritated at being here since he's missing his friends at school. But Mom is concerned—in fact, she's in tears because she heard some gurgling and thrashing in her son's bedroom the previous night and found him in the middle of a grand mal seizure. Even though the seizure looked serious, it ended after a minute or two. Then the boy went quickly back to sleep and didn't remember anything at breakfast the next morning.

His neurological examination was completely normal, and there was nothing in his past medical history to suggest a neurological problem. His EEG showed the classic features of this kind of benign focal epilepsy, so I didn't even bother with an MRI or medications. MRI scans are always normal with this epilepsy, and the event wasn't threatening in any way. Of course, if anything changed after that and other evidence were presented that didn't fit this type of epilepsy, we would proceed with further testing.

Childhood Absence Epilepsy (Petit Mal)

Childhood absence epilepsy tends to start in school-age children. The absence seizures, or staring spells, usually last ten seconds or so and may occur several times per day. They're commonly referred to as petit mal. About one-third of children with absence epilepsy will also have generalized tonic-clonic seizures (also called grand mal seizures).

During these absence seizures, a child usually exhibits a fixed, blank stare and appears motionless. Sometimes his eyes will roll up briefly, and there may also be twitching at the corners of the mouth or of the eyelids. Certain automatisms (licking, swallowing) may also be present. This condition is fairly easy to diagnose since it can often be triggered in a test environment by having the child hyperventilate (by blowing at a pinwheel, for instance). This activity will also bring out the specific abnormality in the EEG, allowing a doctor to identify childhood absence epilepsy with substantial confidence.

Absence seizures typically start and stop abruptly. During the seizure, the child is not aware of what's going on around him. Otherwise, these children are usually normal, intellectually and in other ways.

Certain medications are very effective for absence seizures. Since most children outgrow this form of epilepsy, the medications can often be concluded after a few years.

Juvenile Myoclonic Epilepsy

This epilepsy usually appears in the second decade of life, but it can occur earlier in childhood or young adulthood. It manifests in the form of myoclonic seizures—sudden and spontaneous muscle jerks affecting the shoulders and arms, and sometimes the lower extremities—occurring in isolated events or in clusters.

Jerking often occurs within an hour or so after an individual rises from sleep, and sometimes when the person is tired at the end of the day. The arm jerks may make it difficult to drink from a cup or put on makeup early in the morning, but since the jerking disappears during the day, the epilepsy is often not identified until the individual has a grand mal seizure.

Triggers for juvenile myoclonic epilepsy include sleep deprivation, early awakening, and consumption of alcohol. So the typical behavior of college students—partying late and getting up early for class—can sometimes provoke seizures in people with this type of epilepsy. Some of these patients are also sensitive to strobe lights or vivid computer games, and seizures can occur at pubs and bars or other entertainment venues that young adults may be visiting.

A clear EEG pattern and a predictable set of symptoms often make it easy to diagnose this epilepsy type. Medications usually work well to treat and control this condition, which usually lasts throughout a person's lifetime.

Infantile Spasms

Infantile spasms are a particular seizure type that usually emerges in the first or second year of a child's life. The spasms tend to appear in clusters for several minutes, especially when the child is making the transition into or out of sleep.

The symptoms (also noted on pages 28–29) include:

- Flexing or extending of the trunk, arms, and legs
- Bending forward with the arms and legs extended in the classic diver's posture
- A mixture of the actions described above
- Eye deviation (looking to the right or left unnaturally), another common symptom

The spasms typically either conclude or eventually change into some other type of seizure pattern. An EEG test will show a particular abnormal pattern that is usually easy to see during a routine recording. The medicines used to treat these spasms include some that are rarely used later in life, such as hormone shots. There are many different causes of infantile spasms, so children with this problem will usually undergo testing (MRI, genetic, and biochemical testing) to try to determine the cause.

Take Action

This chapter describes some of the more common forms of pediatric epilepsy. But since the classic features of a specific syndrome are often not present in every individual, not everyone will be diagnosed with a particular epilepsy syndrome. Don't be concerned if the diagnosis is simply "epilepsy." This doesn't necessarily mean that your child's epilepsy will be lifelong or difficult to control.

Lennox-Gastaut Syndrome

Some physicians use the term *Lennox-Gastaut syndrome* to describe children with multiple seizure types and a specific EEG pattern. It has been observed that many children with these two features also have multiple physical and mental handicaps as well as epilepsy that is difficult to control.

However, it's clear that not every child with multiple seizure types and a specific EEG pattern will have multiple handicaps and epilepsy that is difficult to control. This is why some feel that the term Lennox-Gastaut is not useful and paints too bleak a picture for any individual child. Some patients with these seizure types and EEG patterns respond positively to medications and do well in other endeavors. So it's important for any parents whose child is diagnosed with Lennox-Gastaut syndrome to make sure they're receiving full medical options from their health care providers in order to maximize every possible favorable outcome.

Causes of Childhood Epilepsy

People of any age can have epileptic seizures, but there are some causes that are particularly prevalent in children. Among the most common causes of childhood epilepsy are:
- Brain injuries at birth

- Brain malformations

- Benign or malignant brain tumors

- Trauma

- Infection

- Genetic problems that affect brain function

The amount of testing required to diagnose a child with seizures is tailored to the circumstances of each child and is based on what we know from the medical history and a physical examination. For example, we may know that there was a stroke at birth, or meningitis. Or there might have been a car crash in which the infant suffered a severe injury or coma.

But it's good to bear in mind that previous minor head trauma (a child falling off a sofa and bumping his head) is probably unrelated to the epilepsy. In addition, in most cases it's unlikely that anything the mother did or experienced during the pregnancy—with the exception of serious situations involving drug or alcohol abuse, or significant maternal injury or illness—caused the epileptic seizures in her child.

Take Action

A mother may always have unspoken worries that something she did during or after pregnancy might have been a cause of her child's epilepsy. If so, she should discuss these worries with her child's physician, who can usually ease her mind about such concerns. Although it's normal for parents, and especially mothers, to blame themselves, it's also vital that they put these worries behind them and avoid any unnecessary suffering on that score. In short, they must speak up!

Treatment of Epilepsy in Children

The choice of antiseizure drugs and the way they're used is different for children than for adults. For instance, we don't often treat a child's first seizure with medication since the seizure may be an isolated event that won't be repeated. Also, we usually don't treat febrile seizures or benign focal seizures since they're low risk and do not call for drug intervention.

For most other types of epilepsy in children, drug treatment is recommended. Once a drug therapy has been selected by the child's physician, there are dose-related issues to consider. The capacity of a child's body to break down the drug and use it properly changes continually as he grows and develops. The doctor will sometimes check blood levels to make sure the child is taking the proper dosage for his age, weight, and so forth.

Of course, drugs have age-related side effects that must be considered when a program of medication is initiated for any child. Learning and behavior concerns are paramount in children, and your doctor will be looking out carefully for any responses to drug treatment that may affect those areas. Side effects involving hypersensitivity reactions (usually rashes) and appetite suppression or stimulation are often critical factors with children—not to mention reproductive issues with adolescents—and must be monitored closely.

One factor that complicates childhood side effects has to do with the fact that many times a child won't report an unusual condition, such as double vision, as readily as an adult would. Extra attention must be paid to a child's responses. Make sure that you're not missing any side effects that result from communication limitations.

In infants and children, as with adults, epilepsy surgery may be a beneficial form of treatment if drug therapy isn't effective. Surgery may be indicated at almost any age when the source of the epilepsy is situated in a way that would make surgery effective and relatively low risk.

For some children, the ketogenic diet and vagus nerve stimulation can also be effective.

Multiple Conditions

Some children may have other issues coexisting with their epilepsy, such as learning, behavior, or motor problems, which must be treated along with the seizures. In addition, an underlying genetic or metabolic problem will affect not only the brain but other organs as well. In such cases, a multidisciplinary team is the best approach to charting the optimum course of treatment for the child.

It is well to remember that most children with epilepsy are completely healthy in every other way. Once the seizures are controlled through medication, a child with epilepsy can be as normal as any other child.

Parental Concerns about the Future

It's natural for every parent to be concerned about a child's future, and that concern is magnified when seizures are an issue. Will the youngster grow up and be able to live on her own? Will she be able to pursue the career of her choice? Will she have her own family?

It's difficult to predict the future, but we can say that if there are no coexisting problems—if the child is fully functioning when the epilepsy starts—and the seizures can be controlled, the prospects for the child are quite positive. In the face of persisting seizures and coexisting motor or learning problems, the long-term outcome is more guarded. Remember, though, that doctors don't have crystal balls, and your child's full potential will have to reveal itself over time.

Take Action

It's a good idea to seek out support groups in your area for parents of children with epilepsy. Such a group can help you air your concerns and give you insight into how other parents are coping with their child's condition. If there's no such group, talk with your neurologist and see whether you're being too careful (or not careful enough) in handling your child's activities. Sometimes an outside observer, whether a professional or not, can lend a valuable perspective to your situation.

Another issue for parents of epileptic children is how to be neither overprotective of their children nor put them into situations where injury could occur as the result of an ill-timed seizure. The best guideline is to establish reasonable safety conditions for your child and then relax.

Issues at Three Stages of Childhood

Infants and Toddlers

Jonathan
Baby Jonathan was a beautiful infant, perfectly formed and with no known problems. But at six weeks, he began having seizures. The MRI showed a malformation in a focal area of the brain. Drugs stopped the seizures, but Jonathan's parents were devastated to learn that their son wasn't completely normal. While the parents were justifiably concerned about their son's future, the malformation was not extensive.

Take Action

Check to see whether your infant or toddler is meeting age-appropriate milestones for cognitive and motor development, and alert your doctor if those milestones aren't being achieved. Also inquire about special early stimulation programs that your child can attend to augment his developmental progress.

So far, Jonathan is normal in all other ways, and the malformation appears to be in a noncritical area of the brain. There is much reason for optimism about his developmental progress remaining on track. However, it's impossible to resolve all the questions about Jonathan's future this early in life. Difficult as it is, we'll have to wait and see how things develop before we know all the answers.

In the case of infants and toddlers, a key concern is cognitive and motor development, and our goal is to maximize development in both those areas. Medication, seizures, and underlying conditions can all contribute to hampering the infant's progress across the board.

School-Age Children

Morgan

When it comes to high-energy nine-year-old girls, Morgan was the perfect example. Even though she had had seizures since she was small, her few mild seizures per year were under control, and Morgan kept active in sports and the Girl Scouts. But now that she wanted to go off to summer camp, her mother and father were worried about her safety. Her parents got in touch with the camp nurse and discussed Morgan's situation, arranging for some special supervision, especially for swimming and horseback riding. As a result, the parents felt comfortable in sending their daughter off to Camp Chippewa.

Prominent issues in this age range involve making sure the child is integrated into the school environment, developing skills for social interaction with the other kids, and handling the academic assignments. Emotional stability and safety become more important at this age since as the child grows, she will want to exert more independence.

For example, a bicycle rider should always wear a helmet and ought to ride on a quiet side street where the risk of injury would be minimized if a seizure should occur. Other areas of concern include swimming and bathing and climbing trees or ladders.

Just remember that we don't want kids to be sedentary and overprotected; we want them out and active and involved in their schools and communities. Try to make sure that the lines of communication stay open so that the child can confide any fears or frustrations he might have when facing teasing at school or in the neighborhood. And seek out ways to inform classmates and friends about his condition. It will aid acceptance.

Teenagers

Jacob

Jacob was having a blast as a junior in high school, except for the hassle of having to take his medications every day. His mother was constantly on his case about his drug therapy, and it made him feel like a little boy. After much arguing, Jacob's mother finally let him take over the management of his medication. But soon after, Jacob had a grand mal seizure.

The truth came out when hospital blood tests showed that he had no medication in his system. We asked when he had stopped taking his pills, and Jacob admitted that it had been several weeks earlier. We came to an agreement that his mother would be involved with his medication as he got back on his drug-therapy routine. And his driving privileges were suspended for a month until he was stabilized. (Usually, there's at least a six-

month waiting period for driving privileges to be reinstated after a seizure. But seizures resulting from interruption of medication are a special case, and driving can often be restarted shortly after stabilizing the drug therapy.) Now Jacob has a clearer understanding of how important his medication is to maintaining the independent life he wants so much.

Whether seizures are being controlled, as Jacob's were before he took himself off medication, or are less controlled, epilepsy can pose unique challenges for teens. Peer relationships and independence are vital for adolescents. They don't want to have epilepsy and are often angry and frustrated with the limitations imposed by the condition.

It can be hard work to help teenagers with epilepsy become confident and self-sufficient, especially if their seizures aren't controlled and the blossoming young adults have to deal with the challenges caused by these events. These challenges can include social problems, the inability to drive a car, and other issues.

Sometimes teens simply forget to take their medications. Sometimes, as adolescents are likely to do, they feel immortal. Sometimes they're tired of following rules and procedures. In some cases, teens want to take control of their medications, and that can work out very well. In other cases, the teen needs a parent's help to stay on track.

I often tell my adolescent patients that it's their responsibility to make sure they take their medications as prescribed. But I still want their parents involved. The team approach usually works best, especially for high school students who get wrapped up in their busy lives.

The good news is that most people with epilepsy, including teenagers, can blend into society, and most people will never know they have the condition. It just requires parents to be creative and good communicators with their children.

What You Should Know

- While a child may have any of the same seizure types as an adult, there are special epilepsies that affect only the young.

- Fortunately, some childhood epilepsies often disappear as children grow older.

- Some childhood epilepsies respond best to certain medications, and one benign type of epilepsy usually requires no medication at all.

- Children of different ages have very different attitudes toward their epilepsy, and this must be taken into account when they're being helped through their treatment process.

Chapter 8

Epilepsy in Seniors

Now that the baby boomers are entering their 60s, seniors are becoming the fastest growing segment of the U.S. population. And the number of seniors with epilepsy is going up, not just because there are more people in this age category, but also because they're more susceptible than younger people to strokes, brain tumors, and other events that cause epilepsy.

Treatment with antiepileptic medication requires special attention in seniors. Compared to younger individuals, seniors are often more sensitive to medication side effects at lower doses. Toby's experience illustrates this point.

Toby
Toby was quite an accomplished amateur boxer in his younger days. Dubbed "Toby the Tornado," he won the Golden Gloves at age 18 and then boxed successfully during his stint in the army. After retiring from his career as

a TV scriptwriter, the still-athletic Toby heard about a new fitness craze called boxing aerobics, in which both men and women participated. Combining the bouncing footwork of a boxer in combination with jabs and roundhouse swings, the sport was fast becoming a popular way to maintain and increase fitness.

This was right up his alley. Within a few months, Toby was teaching a class in boxing aerobics at his local YMCA. A year later, he opened his own mini-gym, where he taught classes to students ranging from teenagers to a couple of feisty 80-somethings. Seeing upwards of 50 people a day in small and large groups, Toby was feeling great and loving the idea of using his boxing expertise to help others stay fit.

However, out of the blue one day, Toby had a seizure at home. His wife reported that his left arm started jerking and then he passed out, with his arms and legs jerking. He woke up in the ambulance with a headache and blood in his mouth from biting his tongue.

At the hospital, even though his EEG and MRI showed no abnormality, I decided to treat this first seizure with medication. I was worried about the likelihood that another seizure would follow, and I wanted to make sure that Toby would continue pursuing the life he enjoyed so much.

A few days later, as that drug was working its way into Toby's system, he had another milder seizure, with jerking of the left arm but no loss of consciousness. This episode established without question that he was certainly a candidate for drug therapy.

Toby jumped back in the boxing ring with both feet, teaching his classes as usual, with his wife driving him to and from the gym. But a few weeks later, he realized that his coordination was off and he wasn't able to demonstrate shift-and-shuffle footwork as he had been doing. Also, he *noticed that his energy and motivation weren't as high as they had been in the recent past.*

Toby felt another change as well, one that was interfering with his love of Shakespeare. Ever since college, Toby had been in love with the language of the plays and sonnets. He had memorized many of the bard's poems and speeches from his plays and could recite them for hours. He was famous for sharing these classics with friends and family—not to mention his students, between right uppercuts. But now he was having trouble remembering the lines, and when he did remember, sometimes his words were slurred.

Although no one else picked up on these fairly minor symptoms, Toby was concerned enough to ask me about them. Fortunately, when I examined him and spoke with him further, I didn't find any evidence of something new and serious happening to him, such as a stroke. I reviewed his medication and saw that some of his symptoms might result from either the drugs or the dosages as prescribed. After I switched him to a different drug at a lower dose, Toby was seizure-free for six months. This delighted his wife, since at that point she didn't have to drive him back and forth to the gym anymore. As for Toby, he was again floating like a butterfly in the ring and, during breaks, regaling his students with a powerful rendition of "The Seven Ages of Man."

Issues for Seniors with Epilepsy

Stroke accounts for up to 80 percent of mature-onset epilepsy. Other causes include brain tumors, head injuries, and Alzheimer's. But very often, the cause of epilepsy in an older person is never known.

It could result from a subtle combination of factors that occur as that person ages.

In the medical community, our focus is on keeping seniors with epilepsy as active as possible, particularly since today's elderly are very involved in their communities and expect more from their lifestyles.

Issues of particular concern for seniors with epilepsy include drug therapy and drug interaction, seizure reporting, and safety and independence.

Drug Therapy and Drug Interaction

When it comes to epilepsy medication, the margin between an effective dose and one that is toxic is often smaller for seniors than for younger persons. Seniors tend to be more sensitive to dose-related side effects, especially those involving balance, coordination, mood, alertness, clarity of thought, and mobility.

In an elderly person, drug toxicity can often set in at lower doses. This means that the average senior has a narrower therapeutic index, and the doctor must be alert to the need to adjust dosage or even to switch to a different medication. Also, it takes seniors longer to clear drugs from their systems since metabolism slows down somewhat with age. As a result, seniors often benefit from a lower dose of medication.

Take Action

For Seniors
If possible, contact a physician who has experience treating seniors with epilepsy so that he can deal with any complications that may arise from the combination of drugs that you're taking.

It's also important that your physician be fully informed of every medication you're taking for any condition. All possible side effects from drug interactions must be considered. And make sure that your doctor gives you a clear and understandable explanation of the possible effects of an interaction between the epilepsy drug he's prescribing and your other medications. If there are certain effects that would be dangerous or debilitating for you and your lifestyle (for example, drowsiness or lack of coordination if you ride a bicycle), be sure to raise this concern so that your physician can respond accordingly.

For Friends and Family of Seniors
If you're a friend or family member of an older person with epilepsy, here are some of the ways you can help:

- Check on the medications he's taking to be sure that all his medical issues, including epilepsy, are being addressed by the prescribed drug therapies.

- All drugs should be on hand for easy access on a regular schedule.

- Make sure that no medications have passed their expiration dates.

- If any drugs are missing, or if there's too large a quantity of any medication (indicating that the patient hasn't been taking them), talk to her and/or her physician to address and correct such lapses.

It's important to respect the senior's privacy and dignity at all times, even as you're attempting to verify that he's taking all his medications. Each situation will pose a different set of concerns. When a senior is alert and involved, like Toby in the previous case history, simply asking about his drug therapy may be sufficient. But for another, a more aggressive approach might be indicated. If so, try not to condescend to the senior or violate his sense of independence. Such sensitivity will contribute to much better relations and a more positive situation.

There's usually a higher risk for complications from drug interactions because many seniors are already taking one or more (perhaps many more) medications to treat other conditions, such as high blood pressure, allergies, pain management, cardiac or other disease, and more. Such interaction side effects will affect the choice of drugs as well as the dosing strategy.

Seizure Reporting Information

Since some seniors live alone or spend significant periods of time by themselves, it may be difficult to get information about seizures from either witnesses or the patient herself. If an elderly person has a seizure while alone at night, she may know because the sheets and blankets are disheveled, or the bed is wet when she awakens, or she bit her tongue and the pain is an indicator. But milder seizures may pass unnoticed if no one is around to observe the event.

Certain episodes of seizure or drug side effects may go unreported by the senior or be thought to be caused by another condition. As a result, there is compelling need to pay extra attention to elderly people with epilepsy.

Take Action

For Seniors
Always aim for a high quality of life. Don't be willing to settle for less just because you're older. Be sure that you're seeing a physician who understands epilepsy and has a good feeling for the needs of seniors. Your goal is to achieve a combination of the best seizure control and the most satisfying lifestyle.

For Friends and Family of Seniors
One of the keys to helping seniors with epilepsy is to make sure that all lines of communication are open and are being used on a continuing basis. If you're a friend or loved one, stay in contact with the senior and make

your inquiries about all aspects of his life a natural part of your conversation. You may be able to discover certain details that could be valuable in helping a doctor improve the patient's quality of life, not to mention his length of life.

If a senior lives alone and you suspect that he may experience seizure activity, it would be wise to invite him into the home of a relative or friend for a short time to see whether witnesses can determine the existence of the seizures and observe their frequency.

Safety and Independence

Living an independent life and being safe while you do it are issues for everyone at every stage of life. Epilepsy certainly can complicate matters, particularly for seniors. For example, seizures can cause a person to lose driving privileges, which can be a severe blow to feelings of independence and autonomy.

The side effects from epilepsy medications can also contribute to a person's loss of independence, particularly when mobility and cognitive awareness are affected. That's why a doctor will be so focused on controlling the seizures and preventing any significant side effects.

Take Action

If you're a senior with epilepsy and you're having a difficult time adjusting to newly imposed restrictions on your independence, talk with your physician to see whether you can work together to find solutions. For example, many communities have dedicated transportation services that can help you get to the stores and other destinations that you want to visit. And social workers connected with senior centers may help you find creative ways to stay connected to your peers, family, friends, and the world at large.

You and other seniors like you should expect to be able to pursue an active, energetic lifestyle. As with any other health challenge you face, we want to make sure your epilepsy doesn't keep you from participating as fully as possible in all the activities that interest you.

What You Should Know

- For seniors there's a smaller margin between an effective dose of medication and a toxic dose, so it may be necessary for physicians to fine-tune their dosage.

- Drug interactions are of particular concern for seniors, who are often taking other medications for unrelated medical problems.

- Seniors and their friends and family members should try to establish a way to report accurately on any seizures that occur.

- The goal for seniors with epilepsy, as for younger patients, is independence and an active life.

Chapter 9

Epilepsy in Women

Women with epilepsy have special issues to consider in relation to hormones, fertility, contraception, and reproduction. But with careful attention and a little planning, most women with epilepsy can manage these issues successfully, including motherhood.

Take Gwen as an example.

Gwen
Gwen and Christopher had been married for five years and almost everything was sailing along beautifully. Christopher was steadily gaining responsibility and authority as a product manager with a large computer firm, and Gwen was a highly respected librarian. At age 26, she had been living with temporal lobe epilepsy for ten years, but it was well under control.

The one wrinkle in their life was her inability to conceive. They had been trying since their honeymoon in the Bahamas, but nothing had happened. Gwen conscientiously monitored for ovulation and tried to time everything properly, but the whole effort started to feel more like a science project than a romantic interlude, and the two were beginning to feel frustrated.

Gwen's neurologist double-checked her medications to make sure that the drugs weren't having an adverse effect on her ovarian function or fertility. And of course Christopher was also tested to ensure that he was fully functional and potent. The couple then consulted with a fertility specialist, and in cooperation with her neurologist, they decided that Gwen would be a good candidate for fertility-enhancing medication. She began those drugs, and within six months she received the good news that she was pregnant.

When they were three months pregnant, they moved to Cleveland, where Christopher had been relocated by his business. Gwen settled in quickly as an assistant librarian at an East Side library branch and faithfully continued taking her medications. But with the hassle of setting up a new home and getting started at her job, she'd been putting off seeing a new neurologist. Since her pregnancy was progressing without any problems, Gwen felt no urgency about seeing a neurologist immediately.

But on a sunny Wednesday when she was busy with paperwork in a back office of the library, Gwen had a mild breakthrough seizure, her first one in more than seven years.

When I saw her at the hospital, I checked the blood level of the drug she was taking. It was lower than it had been in the past, according to her records, which had been forwarded to us. It appeared that the breakdown of the drug in her body was accelerated by her pregnancy, with factors such as a larger body mass and a sped-up metabolism contributing to the situation.

I increased her dosage and arranged for the medication levels in her blood to be checked again in a few weeks. Then we scheduled monthly visits with blood tests to make sure that Gwen was maintaining the proper amount of medication in her system.

The remainder of her pregnancy proceeded uneventfully. I increased her medication doses several times during the pregnancy to keep the drug efficacy at optimum levels. She had some concern about the possibility of a fetal malformation, but the ultrasound showed no problems. One month before delivery, we put Gwen on vitamin K so that those levels would be built up in the baby. This is done often since some antiepileptic drugs have been known to reduce the ability of the newborn's blood to clot.

Gwen gave birth to a healthy seven-pound girl, whom they named Ashley. At that point, I cut Gwen's dosage to reflect the change that had just occurred in her body. Such a decrease usually prevents the side effects that might occur if the higher pregnancy-level dosage of medication were maintained. That's how it worked for Gwen, who adjusted beautifully to the lower dose.

Gwen, Christopher, and Ashley settled into a normal routine for young families—if a hectic and sleepless routine can be described as normal. Mom and Dad relished their new roles as parents, and a year later, out of the blue, they were delighted to learn that Gwen was pregnant again. Now they're busy preparing for Ashley's new little brother.

Hormones and Epilepsy

When it comes to hormones and epilepsy, it's a two-way street. Hormones can affect the threshold for epileptic seizures, and seizures in turn can change some of the hormonal regulation and control in the body. And since women go through cycles in which their hormonal milieus change on a monthly basis, epilepsy in women is often quite a dynamic process.

Some women with epilepsy tend to have seizures at certain times in their hormonal cycle (called *catamenial-associated seizures*). If there's evidence of such a seizure pattern, it's a good idea for the woman to chart her seizures and her menstrual periods on a calendar. Fortunately, there are some medications that can modulate this kind of seizure activity, and a woman should ask her doctor about these drugs if she finds her seizures occurring in this manner.

In other cases, the seizures can affect a woman's (and a man's) hormones. Since brain structures such as the hypothalamus and the pituitary gland control the production of hormones, the electrical storm of an epileptic seizure can alter hormone production and dispersal. Drugs can also contribute to this hormonal disruption. The results of such hormonal changes in women can include ovulatory dysfunction, ovarian problems, and other issues. Generally, the fertility rates for women with epilepsy are somewhat lower than for women without epilepsy.

Increased body weight and altered menstrual cycles are strong clues to the existence of changed hormonal patterns in a woman with epilepsy.

Many people wonder whether hormonal milestones such as puberty and menopause affect epilepsy in any important way. Indeed, some epilepsies (such as juvenile myoclonic epilepsy) tend to appear at puberty, and others (such as benign focal epilepsy of childhood) disappear around puberty. The effect of puberty on girls with epilepsy is different in different people—seizures can remain the same, grow worse, or lessen in severity.

> **Take Action**
>
> Be sure to let your doctor know about any physical changes related to hormones that might affect your condition or your treatment. In women, these include weight gain, menstrual irregularities, the appearance of new acne, hair loss, or other noticeable bodily changes.

Typically with catamenial-associated seizures, there are two times during the month when vulnerability to seizures is greatest: the time of menstrual flow (and the three days leading up to it) and at ovulation between periods. At these times, levels of estrogen are relatively high and levels of progesterone are relatively low. If you think there may be an association between your seizures and menses, then keep a calendar of these events. This will help your doctor to determine whether specialized treatment approaches may be right for you.

Little is known at this time about the effect, if any, of menopause on epilepsy.

Epilepsy, Sex, and Fertility

Sexual Relations

Epilepsy can have a definite impact on the sex life and fertility of both men and women. Epilepsy can contribute to a less satisfying and less productive sex life for a couple if one or both partners have seizures.

Sexual dysfunction in men and women primarily shows up as diminished sexual desire and an inability to perform. For instance, some epilepsy drugs can lower testosterone in a man, reducing both his fertility and his ability to perform sexually. This reaction is usually physiological, not psychological. Some men with epilepsy report a lack of early morning tumescence. Some women with epilepsy experience reduced desire, difficulty achieving orgasm, or pain with intercourse (sometimes resulting from vaginal dryness).

Of course, for people who have epilepsy, issues of social development may play into problems connected with sexuality. The low self-esteem that sometimes develops in early years can negatively affect a person's ability to perform sexually, even when there are no physical drawbacks.

Note: In rare cases, having intercourse can trigger a seizure in some people with epilepsy. And a small number of people have sexual sensations during seizures that occur at times when no sexual act is taking place, such as at work, while shopping, and during other ordinary activities. Also, epilepsy drugs can have some impact on a person's libido or potency.

Fertility

For physiological reasons, people with epilepsy have a reduced likelihood of having children. Women may have interruptions in their ovulatory and menstrual cycles that can affect their fertility; men may have disturbances of their pituitary gland hormones.

Take Action

If your physician doesn't ask you about your sexual activity, volunteer the information and discuss the ways in which you would like to see

> improvement in that area. To begin with, you should probably have complete neurological and physical exams.
>
> There are many ways to approach solutions to sexual problems brought on by epilepsy. The process should start with your neurologist, who will make sure that the medications currently prescribed aren't creating an obstacle. You may also want to consult with an endocrinologist, gynecologist, or other specialist. Next, you can consult with experts in sexual relations or psychology to see whether there are different approaches you can pursue. While the cause of many of these problems is in part physical, there are usually psychosocial issues that should also be addressed.
>
> Also, there are products available—such as erectile dysfunction medications for men and vaginal lubricants for women—that can make intercourse more comfortable and satisfying.

Contraception and Planning Your Family

The vast majority of children born to mothers who have epilepsy are normal in every way, so a woman's epilepsy is no reason to avoid having children. The risk that a child will have epilepsy is somewhat higher if the mother or father has epilepsy, but the difference is small enough (under 5 percent) that it usually does not play a role in family planning.

Women with epilepsy have many issues to consider as they make their decisions about whether to have children. But with careful preparation and a little foresight, a woman with epilepsy can plan her family as successfully as any other woman.

Women using hormonal contraception find that some antiepileptic drugs can undermine the effectiveness of birth control pills, patches, or shots. So in some cases, unexpected or breakthrough pregnancies are possible unless the woman takes higher doses of birth control pills or uses barrier methods. If pregnancy isn't part of your plans, it's a good idea to consult your doctor about shifting away from the drugs that have a negative effect on the efficacy of birth control pills.

On the other hand, sometimes birth control pills can speed up the clearance of an antiepileptic drug from the bloodstream so that breakthrough seizures are possible. Before starting on birth control pills, ask your neurologist if they'll have any effect on your epilepsy medication (and vice versa), and make the necessary adjustments. In some cases, periodic intramuscular injections of medroxyprogesterone, or Depo-Provera, may be more favorable for contraception.

Take Action

- For couples who are having difficulty becoming pregnant, it may be wise to consult a fertility specialist, who can suggest the best way to proceed.

- Your neurologist may be able to adjust your antiepileptic medications.

- Many technologies, such as in vitro fertilization, may be appropriate in overcoming fertility problems.

In light of all the complex interactions involving hormones and birth control pills, an IUD (intrauterine device) might be an excellent choice for contraception. These devices are much safer, more effective, and easier to use than in the past, and they prevent the complications that can arise from drug interactions.

When you want to become pregnant, you should first meet with your neurologist to review all the factors involved. She can help maximize the chances of a completely normal pregnancy resulting in a healthy baby. Some minor, hard-to-detect "cosmetic" malformations can occur, and the risk of birth defects (spina bifida, congenital heart defect, cleft lip or palate) increases with the amount of antiepileptic drugs used. Therefore, it is wise to cut back to just one drug, if possible, before getting pregnant. And the drug you choose should be one that's less likely to contribute to birth defects. Supplementation with vitamins, such as folic acid, is also important to reduce the risk of birth defects.

Don't wait until you know you're pregnant before making changes to your drug therapy. When malformations occur in the fetus, they happen very early, even before you're aware that you're pregnant. It's critical to plan for a pregnancy and make all necessary adjustments to medications before conception is attempted. You and your doctor may decide to reduce or go off drugs entirely before conception if the seizures have been well controlled for a significant period of time.

Take Action

Always supplement your diet with multivitamins and folic acid long before you make any plans to have a baby. And make sure that your team—which could include a neurologist, OB/GYN, pediatrician, and in some cases, a geneticist—is in place with all members working toward the same goal.

Pregnancy

Most women with epilepsy have normal pregnancies. Monthly checkups are important to make sure that the doctor can make adjustments in medications to compensate for the changes going on in the woman's body. Usually, the medications have to be increased during pregnancy to maintain the same blood levels and seizure protection.

We want to control the seizures since some of this activity, especially grand mal seizures, could adversely affect the fetus. Ultrasound scans made during the pregnancy, even those performed for other reasons, can often provide reassuring evidence that no birth defects have occurred.

In the postpartum period, drug doses usually need to be reduced to the prepregnancy level. A woman should have her blood levels checked two weeks after childbirth and then six to ten weeks later to make certain that medication levels have resumed their baseline profiles.

Epilepsy and Baby Care

Once mother and baby are back home and everyone is doing well, the mother may want to breast-feed her baby. Even though the antiepileptic drugs do find their way into the breast milk, babies seem to do well with it. So we encourage breast-feeding.

Take Action

When feeding your baby, sit in a comfortable and secure chair that affords good support to your back. To avoid unnecessary falls, diaper your baby on the floor, using a changing pad. Be sure there are duplicate baby-care items on every floor of your house to minimize climbing stairs. And when you're moving your baby around the house, as well as outdoors, use a small stroller instead of carrying the infant. By applying common sense, you can avoid many pitfalls and enjoy your baby's early years to the fullest.

In a new mother who has epilepsy, normal sleep deprivation can increase the chances of seizures. If seizures continue, the mother may want to take special precautions when handling her baby in certain situations. For example, the mother may want someone else to be present when she's bathing the baby.

What You Should Know

- Women's (and men's) hormones can affect epilepsy, and vice versa, with the effects varying widely from individual to individual.

- In connection with sexual relations, there are many ways to deal with the problems that epilepsy can pose. Expert guidance can help significantly.

- Armed with proper foresight and preparation, a woman with epilepsy can plan her family as successfully as any other woman.

- A woman with epilepsy should have her medication levels monitored carefully during and after pregnancy to ensure that she's receiving the optimum dosage.

Part Four

Living with Epilepsy

Chapter 10

Mental, Psychological, and Social Challenges

A person living with epilepsy faces many challenges, and they can appear at any stage of life. Though they may seem daunting, there are always ways to handle them and live the life you choose. Here are some suggestions for coping and thriving in these situations.

We are learning that depression may be one of these challenges. Take Rick as an example.

Rick

Among all the excellent salespeople at Drummon Industries, Rick was legendary. Slender, upbeat, and friendly to all, "Rick the Stick" was considered a hall-of-fame talent. He held down a territory that encompassed large parts of three Midwestern states, and his annual sales figures for commercial plumbing fixtures were always increasing. Some of his coworkers jokingly accused him of driving a secondhand NASCAR vehicle because of the way he managed to race here and there, squeezing so many sales calls into the average week.

So when he had a grand mal seizure at age 34, it was a devastating blow to Rick's career and to his sense of worth. It was especially difficult when he learned that he wouldn't be allowed to drive until six seizure-free months had passed. Owing to the nature of his work, which depended on driving, we put him on drugs immediately to try to prevent another seizure.

Unfortunately, a month later Rick had another seizure. It was milder, but he still lost awareness and had some automatisms. That meant that he had to reset the clock and begin a new six-month waiting period. We increased his medication dosage with the intent of avoiding any further seizures. Unfortunately, Rick continued to have occasional seizures no matter what medications he tried.

To add to his problems, stresses at home were mounting as his wife, Darlene, and their three children tried to adjust to the consequences of this new reality. Rick's employer was understanding and encouraged him to continue selling over the phone, but it just wasn't the same, and his sales fell off markedly. Even though the family finances were fine for the short term, Rick began worrying about his long-range financial future.

Soon, his family noticed that Rick was becoming more irritable about things that had never bothered him before. He was short-tempered with the kids and Darlene, and soon he was just sitting around the house, unable to muster interest in anything. This behavior was very unlike the Rick that Darlene knew and loved, so she called his neurologist to ask about the apparent deterioration in Rick's behavior.

After consultation, his neurologist and a psychologist agreed that Rick was experiencing depression, which is not an uncommon circumstance for people with epilepsy. He was put on antidepressant medication, and after more testing, it was determined that Rick was a good subject for temporal lobe epilepsy surgery. This procedure could remove the damaged part of his brain affected by his hippocampal sclerosis, and we hoped it would control his seizures permanently.

Surgery appeared to be the best course. Even though Rick's seizures weren't too severe or frequent, they had an enormous impact on his life and his psychological wellbeing. The surgery was successful, and six months later, Rick was back on the road again. Things were looking up, and under the guidance of his doctor, Rick gradually stopped his antidepressant medication.

Over the next few months, even though his seizures appeared to be under control, Rick began to feel a little down in the dumps. This surprised him, but he couldn't help the way he felt. So the antidepressant medication was reinstated, and Rick is now much more his old self. And his sales numbers once again are raising appreciative eyebrows all around his company.

The Mental, Psychological, and Social Challenges of Epilepsy

Cognitive Challenges

Most people with epilepsy have normal intelligence, and some have extraordinary cognitive abilities. Still, some individuals with epilepsy have problems to a greater or lesser degree with memory or learning, compared to people of a similar age and level of education who don't have epilepsy.

Take Action

If you notice any dulling of your thinking or memory, raise this issue with your physician. He may be able to either adjust the dosage or change medications to help avoid these cognitive problems.

Also, there are some psychologists who have expertise in devising coping mechanisms for people with memory difficulties. They can help you develop strategies, such as making lists of various tasks and obligations, that can enable you to navigate through your day with a minimum of disruption.

If you're the parent of a child with learning problems and epilepsy, you may want to talk with her teachers. The youngster may benefit from an individualized educational program based on the results of neuropsychological testing.

Cognitive difficulties can be caused by a number of different factors, which include:

- The underlying source of the epilepsy

- Drug side effects

- Frequent (daily) seizures that interrupt normal thought processes

But the impact of epilepsy on cognition is so variable and individualized that it's impossible to reliably predict how epilepsy may affect a person's thought processes.

Psychiatric Issues

Depression. Depression is the most frequent mental disorder occurring in people with epilepsy. The prevalence of depression among patients with controlled seizures is 10 to 20 percent, and 20 to 60 percent in people with hard-to-manage epilepsy. It's vitally important for the patient, his family, and friends to pay attention to this sometimes life-threatening condition. Indeed, the rate of suicide for people with epilepsy is ten times that of the general population, and it's the leading cause of death for people in this category.

> **Take Action**
>
> Be sure you remain in close contact with your neurologist, who will recognize any signs of depression and address them immediately. Medications and/or psychological counseling can often help a person deal with the limitations imposed by epilepsy and related issues.

Symptoms of depression can vary, of course, from person to person, but among the most noticeable are feelings of hopelessness, general anxiety and fear, and irritability.

Unfortunately, it's often easy to ignore or minimize the symptoms of depression in people with epilepsy since their behaviors and feelings might be automatically and mistakenly expected of someone who is medically challenged. ("No wonder she's sad, she has epilepsy.")

Depression and epilepsy need not go hand in hand. A person with epilepsy who exhibits the symptoms of depression must seek professional counseling. Some antiepileptic drugs can exacerbate depression, while other antiepileptic medications help to reduce these feelings.

Anxiety. The unpredictability of seizures or drug side effects can contribute to anxiety reactions in people with epilepsy. The anxiety can take the form of panic attacks or obsessive-compulsive behaviors. But the most common manifestation is a generalized anxiety disorder (exaggerated worry and tension when there's little or nothing to provoke those feelings) that happens between seizures. The prevalence of anxiety disorders in patients with epilepsy varies widely.

Take Action

Since seizures and panic attacks often appear similar, it's important to try to distinguish between the two behaviors so that the correct condition can be identified and treated. Conversation with your neurologist can usually sort out the differences, but additional EEGs can sometimes be helpful. Medications and psychotherapy can help alleviate anxiety disorder.

Aggression. While aggressive behavior is rare during a seizure, such behavior may be noted after a seizure occurs. At times, aggression is unleashed in response to attempts by witnesses to physically restrain the person during or after the seizure. There also may be some hallucinations or confusion present to cause this violent lashing out.

Certain drugs may also contribute to aggressive and irritable behavior unrelated to the actual seizures.

Take Action

Do not restrict the movement of an epileptic person during recovery from a seizure, especially one who has demonstrated aggressive tendencies after previous seizures. If aggression or irritability is a problem in the periods between seizures, consult with a neurologist to consider the possibility of a drug side effect.

Living in the World

Sports and Other Recreational Activities: Risk-Benefit Decisions

People with epilepsy are as interested as other people are in sports, hobbies, and recreations of every sort. But the decision to take part in a given activity is more complicated for them than it is for people without epilepsy and calls for more forethought. The benefits of participating must be weighed against the risks.

Obviously, an activity should be considered carefully for its risk to the person with epilepsy as well as to other people who might be in the area if a seizure should occur. Skydiving would pose a serious risk, while archery would be much less dangerous since the only moment of risk takes place when the bowstring is pulled back.

People with epilepsy are encouraged to engage in sports because they're enjoyable, they're an accepted means of social interaction, and they keep people healthy. But it would be wise to pursue low-risk sports such as running, cross-country skiing, or tennis, rather than high-risk sports such as skydiving or scuba diving.

Other factors that affect this risk-benefit decision include drug side effects, the proper use of safety equipment, and the availability of supervision or help from fellow participants in the event of a seizure.

Driving

It's a fact that a person with epilepsy can become involved in an auto accident if a seizure should occur when he's behind the wheel. Nevertheless, it's difficult to gauge the likelihood of vehicle crashes caused by epileptic seizures since there's little reliable data on such incidents.

> **Take Action**
>
> Ask your neurologist about the rules in your state that address the circumstances of people with epilepsy who wish to drive. Your doctor can be your partner in the effort to help you drive safely and legally. Comprehensive discussions of epilepsy and driving can be found at:
>
> - The transportation page for Epilepsy.com—the website for the Epilepsy Therapy Project: www.epilepsy.com/epilepsy/social_driving.html
>
> - The Epilepsy Foundation's transportation information site: www.epilepsyfoundation.org/living/wellness/transportation
>
> In general, people with epilepsy who are passengers on airplanes, trains, buses, and other public transportation have the same rights as anyone else. If a seizure occurs in any of those places, it should be handled as it would be anywhere else.

Generally speaking, if a person has been seizure-free for six months, that's a fairly good sign that a seizure-related accident is unlikely. As a result, many states allow people with epilepsy to drive a car once six months have passed since their last seizure, as documented by medical records submitted by the applicant and a written statement provided by a doctor. However, as with many other issues involving epilepsy and driving, among the 50 states there are many different regulations pertaining to this issue.

Employment

There are potentially serious ramifications for people with epilepsy in the workplace. To begin with, there's a lower rate of graduation from high school among those with epilepsy. In the United States, the rate of unemployment or underemployment (a person doing a job substantially below his skill or educational level) for persons with epilepsy is quite significant, with poorly controlled epilepsy correlating to higher levels of unemployment. And even when such a person finds a job, discrimination may result if the epilepsy becomes known.

Take Action

If you're in a job or are pursuing employment for a specific job, review the ADA to determine what your rights are under the law. It is then your decision whether to discuss your condition with your current or prospective employer and determine how to handle your epilepsy with little or no negative impact on the business. With so many different jobs and epilepsy profiles that vary widely, it's impossible to make a blanket recommendation.

An excellent summary of ideas for employees with epilepsy can be found at the website of the U.S. Department of Labor's Job Accommodation Network at *www.jan.wvu.edu/media/epil.htm*.

If you're looking for employment, vocational and career counselors in your area may be of assistance. And two government websites can be of great help to persons with epilepsy who are seeking work:

- The U.S. Department of Education offers a state-by-state listing of state vocational rehabilitation agencies: *http://wdcrobcolp01.ed.gov/Programs/EROD/org_list.cfm*

- The U.S. Department of Labor, Office of Disability Employment Policy, offers additional information:

> www.dol.gov/odep/pubs/fact/laws.htm
>
> If necessary, find out from the Social Security Administration what regulations define qualification for disability payments so that you can receive the financial support you deserve from the government: www.ssa.gov/disability.

The good news is that the Americans with Disabilities Act (ADA) is the law of the land, and it can help people with epilepsy get a job and then hold onto that job as long as reasonable accommodation can be made. Of course, every job presents a different set of workplace conditions that might be affected by the onset of a seizure, so these situations must be addressed on an individual basis. While a person with epilepsy isn't entitled to take any job she desires, even if she qualifies in every other way, there are more opportunities now, thanks to the ADA.

SUDEP (Sudden Unexpected Death in Epilepsy)

We are all aware that we may pass away unexpectedly in any given year, but for some persons with epilepsy this risk may be increased. It is important to remember that in most cases the risk is low, and that the best way to keep the risk as low as possible is to maintain the best possible seizure control. Bringing this topic up with your doctor may be a good way to be sure that you have all the facts, and help put any concerns into perspective.

Social Relationships—Casual and Intimate

Epilepsy can complicate relationships, but it certainly need not cause any relationships to end or change in a negative way. In one-to-one friendships, the first step is to determine how close the relationship is or may become. Is the other person likely to witness a seizure (as an intimate partner would or a close friend)? Much depends on the frequency of your seizures, to be sure, but you can still group your relationships in this way.

In dealing with people who will probably witness a seizure at some point, honesty and openness are the best policies. People tend to be afraid of things they don't understand, so explain your particular condition and put your friends at ease about what happens during a seizure and after. (One good step: Share this book with them and highlight the areas that apply particularly to you and your epilepsy.)

If you're dating someone and the relationship seems to be growing closer, you may want to think about broaching the subject of your epilepsy. Follow your gut instinct about the right time for this discussion, and then be completely honest and confident in presenting the facts. The more you seem to be hiding something or embarrassed or ashamed, the more the other person will pick up on those emotions and feel unsure. You may want to pursue couples therapy at some point, so that a third party can help you both through this process.

It's natural to worry about having a seizure in a public place or in front of other people. But don't avoid going out to theaters, restaurants, school, stadiums, and other such venues. The unpredictability of epilepsy can be challenging, but it shouldn't prevent you from living a full and satisfying life.

What You Should Know

- While most people with epilepsy have normal intelligence, some individuals tend to have problems with memory or learning.

- Depression is a frequent and potentially dangerous complication for people with epilepsy, and it must be treated quickly and aggressively.

- There are always decisions to be made concerning which jobs and activities are safe for people with epilepsy to engage in. Always seek the advice of a neurologist if there's uncertainty in this area.

- A person with epilepsy has rights under the Americans with Disabilities Act (ADA). Be sure you are protecting your rights in terms of employment and in all other aspects of your life.

- In close relationships, honesty about your epilepsy is always the best policy.

Conclusion

Persons with epilepsy and their loved ones no longer need to hide in the shadows. By seeking information and taking an active role in your own medical care, you are tackling epilepsy for yourself and others. Never before in history have so many effective treatments been available to control seizures, and in some cases, even cure the epilepsy altogether. The medical discipline of epilepsy has come a long way, and knowing your options is the first step to making sure that you benefit from these advances.

Even the most advanced treatments, though, aren't yet enough in every case. Some persons continue to live with seizures, despite the best available care at this point in time. For these individuals, new therapies are under development and innovative drugs are entering the pipeline on a continual basis, offering many reasons for optimism.

As epilepsy emerges from the shadows where it has existed for millennia, some of the ways in which the disease is treated are being reconsidered. For instance, it's becoming clear that surgery shouldn't be reserved as a last option. In many cases, surgery can help people with epilepsy achieve a more normal lifestyle much faster than they can by other means.

Also, fresh approaches to the use and selection of antiepileptic drugs may hold the possibility for significant advances in epilepsy treatment. Now that the human genome has been mapped, it may be possible in the future to do a total "genetic scan" of a person.

Such a scan could help us understand an individual's DNA code and thereby assist us in determining which drugs would work best for that person. Known as pharmacogenomics, this emerging medical discipline offers enormous potential for breakthroughs.

For all these reasons, I believe that there's great hope for the future of epilepsy treatment. And that's the best news of all—not just for everyone involved in treating epilepsy, but most important, for the people who have epilepsy and those who care about them.

Printed in Great Britain
by Amazon